> Dear Sandy,
> Thank you for speaking up on behalf of the voiceless and fighting for the pits! They need good people like you in their corner. Hope you enjoy this ride!
> Much respect,
> Michelle Sathe

# Pit Stops 2

*Adventures with Kara*

Michelle Sathe

Pit Stops 2: Adventures with Kara

Copyright © 2012 by Michelle Sathe/Say The Words Press

All rights reserved. No part of this book may be reproduced or transmitted in any form or by any means without written permission of the author.

ISBN 9780985375935

First Edition

Cover photo: Jonathan Pobre

Cover design: Peter Hernandez

Back cover inset photos: Michelle Sathe

Interior design: Michelle Sathe

All interior photos by Michelle Sathe (with the exception of photos by Denise Martin on pages 8 and 163, Angela Johnson on page 101, Rose Tremblay on page 66 and Erica Daniel on page 164).

Printed in the United States of America

*$1 from each copy of Pit Stops 2 will benefit*
*AngelDogsFoundation.*
*For more information, visit www.angeldogsfoundation.org*

## *Dedications:*

To Wayde Dyer, my alpha dog, for supporting me even when you don't understand.

To Kyle Harris, for trusting me with the precious Chunk…you set the bar for advocates everywhere.

To Carol DeBear and Bonnie Witten, for seeing something special in Kara and making a huge difference for Lancaster's shelter dogs.

To April Lund, Leeanne Shinn, Yvonne Allbee, Jason Griego, Beth Diehl and Laura Chesler for your friendship, support, empathy and inspiration.

To Stephanie M., Gail K., and Ronni W., I couldn't trudge this road without you.

To Lisa Tipton, for starting me on my next chapter and for diligently hacking away at the roots of the homeless pet crisis.

To Margo's Bark and Jen Carle, for sponsoring this adventure and believing in us.

To The Courtad and Gaither families, as well as my parents Jim and Rosie, for giving us a taste of home on the road.

To all the incredible rescuers, volunteers, advocates and shelter workers we met on our journey. You are my heroes.

To Buster and Sam, for letting mama take time away from you to help less fortunate dogs.

To Kara, for showing the world how wonderful pit bulls can be. I'm forever proud to be your aunt.

# Foreword

One would assume that my outlook on the general perception of pit bulls would often be negative. After all, my organization, Downtown Dog Rescue, concentrates our efforts of rescuing dogs and doing outreach primarily in neighborhoods that struggle with the challenges of gang violence and high rates of unemployment. Places where dogs run in packs on the street and most people would not stop to pick up a stray dog, especially a pit bull.

Quite the contrary, I see positive changes every day and it's only getting better.

Sixteen years ago, I really had no idea, good or bad, about what pit bulls were all about until I met my first one, Iron Head, who lived on the street with his person Benny. Honestly, I never gave much thought to what breed Iron Head was. I just thought he was the coolest, smartest dog that I ever met, so why wouldn't other people want dogs like him?

Wow, was I ever wrong. In fact, back in 1996 when I founded DDR, the image of the pit bull might have been at its lowest, most undesirable point. Some shelters wouldn't even adopt this breed out to the public. There were few pit bull advocates and of course, it was the just the beginning of the Internet, which has since had a huge impact on connecting all of the people who care about this breed.

An undeniable change that occurred in the perception of the pit bull terrier was the conviction of Michael Vick in December of 2007. If this had been just another fight bust, without the famous person involved, the dogs would have likely have been euthanized because they would have been deemed "too vicious" and or to have "fighting in their bloodline," making them unsafe to be adopted out to anyone, including rescues. Euthanized and forgotten. People would have rationalized that this was done in the best interest of the dogs, a phrase that I still hear too often. Instead, because this case was in the news every day, the public began to follow the dogs and learn the term "victims of cruelty."

Another significant change happened to me personally in 2007, when my lead dog Clancy came into my life, starving, sick and scarred. He has been called a "Grand Champion" or a "Gladiator" by some of the men in the community where we offer free spay/neuter and support to promote owner retention. I see Clancy as a victim of animal cruelty, who has now become the dog that he was always supposed to be. Because the public is more open to seeing these types of dogs, due to the publicity that surrounded the Vick dogs, Clancy is welcomed wherever he goes. As the DDR mascot, a Canine Good Citizen and a certified therapy dog that passed his test at 14 years old, Clancy goes everywhere with me. Pretty amazing for a former fighting dog or is it?

Clancy, like every pit bull, is a dog first. As a dog rescue that rescues a lot of pit bull type dogs, it's important to keep this belief front and center, avoiding a special classification for this breed. Anyone who doesn't believe me that a pit bull type dog can't be categorized into a few words should come down to the DDR kennel when it's play time. There you would see different breeds of dogs playing together, having a great time. Further blowing away the stereotypes of pit bull type dogs, our males play with other males, lots of females play with females, old dogs, young dogs and every age in between. They might be underdogs but they all have a lot of heart.

As far as I'm concerned, the pit bull terrier is America's breed. So why doesn't the whole country embrace the breed and stop introducing legislation that is breed specific? In my mind it all boils down to one point: lack of education about the breed and about dog care and handling in general. I am truly saddened whenever I hear about the latest "pit bull attack" in the news. 99.9 percent of the time when the pit bull type dog attacked a person, the dog was not sterilized, it was not a family pet and the owner did not have proper control over the dog. A reckless few end up taking the media spotlight from the hundreds of thousands of responsible dog owners, who call a pit bull type dog their family pet.

Therefore, it truly takes a village to keep these inevitable attacks from occurring. If you could walk in my shoes and see dogs that are chained up 24/7 in filthy yards without adequate shelter, dogs that never leave their back yards and are largely forgotten except for someone throwing some food out or the female that is bred back to back to back, producing 12 to 13 puppies per pregnancy, twice a year, for four to five or more years, you might understand why. What chance do these dogs have?

I'm sure that this was a question that Michelle had when first traveling across the country with Loren, writing "Pit Stops." Experiencing breed discrimination firsthand, seeing the "pit bull problem" of too many unwanted pit bulls and not enough adoptions is a nationwide epidemic. So why am I optimistic about the future of the breed?

Downtown Dog Rescue puts a tremendous amount of effort and money into running an outreach program which uses mobile spay/neuter clinics at parks in some of the most underserved communities This is an opportunity for "yard dogs" to get out and off their chains just long enough to get free vaccinations and sterilizations along with a microchip and an invitation to come out to our free dog training class.

The good news is that I do see some of the clinic dogs with their owners out at Sunday training class. There our lead trainer, Cornelius "Dog Man" Austin, shouts out to the entire class of 30 to 40 pit bull owners, "I offer this class free of charge because your mistake with your dog is my mistake is all of our mistakes. Too many of these mistakes and the pit bull will be banned completely." Pretty radical talk but it has scared some of the dog owners into getting more involved with their dogs. I've seen them go from padlocks and chains to martingale collars and a CGC diploma all within six months.

Just like Michelle and Kara changed people's perception at every stop they made, having a well-trained pit bull that is social is what we all need to strive for. We need to continue to show the breed in the most positive way possible. Social change can happen if we all care enough to get into the communities that need us the most, overcoming our fears and frustrations.

Just start the work, even if the work is just one small step to help one dog owner with their dog.

Lori Weise, Founder
Downtown Dog Rescue

# Table of Contents

Introduction: Kara's Angels ................................................................. 1

Rolling Stones ....................................................................................... 11

Back on the Bayou ............................................................................... 28

Lucky Dogs ............................................................................................ 45

Hello Dolly ............................................................................................. 58

The Low Country .................................................................................. 79

B-Town ................................................................................................... 87

Buckets O' Fun ...................................................................................... 98

Outlaws .................................................................................................. 109

Mending Hearts and Helping Pits ..................................................... 117

My Kind of Town .................................................................................. 130

Our Own Private Idaho ....................................................................... 138

Setting an Example .............................................................................. 148

Finding My Way .................................................................................... 160

Epilogue & Resources .......................................................................... 164

## Introduction: Kara's Angels

They say it takes a village to raise a child. It certainly takes the same to rescue a pit bull out of the Los Angeles County shelter system.

The heavily pregnant, stout fawn pit bull with pointy ears was a stray picked up by Animal Control and sent to Lancaster Shelter on October 7, 2010. She was given the ID A4197640 and taken to a small kennel, surrounded by hundreds of barking dogs. Many were pit bulls of every size, shape and color, sometimes two or three to a kennel.

When at capacity, Lancaster Shelter holds up to 500 dogs at a time. Like most shelters, pit bulls are often the first dogs to be put down, usually for space. Every 24 hours Lancaster receives up to 80 stray and owner-surrendered animals while only adopting out about 25 on a good day. Luckily for A4197640, who was eventually named Kara, she had a savior. Carol DeBear, who has volunteered at Lancaster Shelter for more than 10 years, was also a foster with a soft spot for injured, sick or pregnant dogs.

"The first time I met her, Kara was huge, like a hippo, yet her little butt started wiggling. She was just special. There were two pregnant pits and I was supposed to get other one, but I took one look at Kara and said she was going with me," DeBear recalled. "A rescue took the other momma."

Kara temporarily became part of the DeBear home, which has two rooms set aside just for fosters, on October 12, charming its residents with her sweet nature. The dog's golden eyes revealed a soft heart and Kara's little furrowed brow was always creased with concern and curiosity. She'd waddle up to Carol, her husband and the kids, her swollen stomach swaying side to side, determined to give and get regular doses of affection.

On October 27, Kara delivered 11 puppies, one of them stillborn. According to Carol, the maternal role was natural for Kara.

"She was definitely an experienced mama and very attentive. The vet said Kara had probably had several litters and her personality gave us that impression, too," she said. "There's a lot of backyard breeders here, gangbanger types, and her puppies were definitely purebred. Her pregnancy was not an accident."

Weaned and healthy by the holidays, all of Kara's puppies were picked up by local families during a Christmas adoption event hosted by the shelter.

"The puppies were absolutely beautiful and well-socialized. We were very happy that they went so fast," Carol said.

Kara, like a lot of mamas, was left behind. Her nipples were practically hanging to the ground, not an appealing sight to most adopters. Kara cocked her head as the last of her pups was whisked away to a new home, looking at Carol with an even more furrowed brow and concerned expression.

"Mamas are weathered, they're older, they're not cute little foo-foo dogs anymore. Some rescues are willing to help the moms, but a lot of them still get put down," Carol said.

Lancaster Shelter's policy for fosters is to return mother dogs to shelter once puppies are weaned, so they can be put on the adoption floor. Though she had a house full of fosters and her own dogs to consider, Carol refused.

"I wouldn't take Kara back to the shelter until I knew we had someone lined up to take her," Carol said.

\*\*\*

In October 2010, I had released "Pit Stops." It was a long, arduous task writing a book, something entirely different for this instant gratification journalist. It's one thing to crank out an 800 to 1,000 word story every day, quite another to piece together a 70,000 word linear narrative.

When "Pit Stops" came out, I felt a strong sense of pride, especially since I was the one who published it. The book looked really professional. It was so cool to see two years of planning and hard work come to fruition, though now I had the fun task ahead of selling it. Being a control freak, I enjoyed making "Pit Stops" entirely my own, but it also meant acting as publicist, the marketing company, the signing booker and so on.

"Pit Stops" made its debut at Bow-Wows & Meows Pet Fair, where Loren and Stefan came by to celebrate and help me promote it.

True to his word, Stefan had stayed in touch with me, emailing photos of his "Lolo" in a chef's hat, at the farmer's market, or stretched out on his leather couch.

Stefan had worked hard with a trainer on Loren. Eventually she became so dog-tolerant that he rescued another pit bull, this time a pup that was being sold by backyard breeders at the park near his apartment. When Stefan threatened to call the cops, the pit bull purveyors handed over the little black puppy, whom he named Lacey.

Originally, Stefan was going to foster Lacey until she found a new home. But I could see from his Facebook posts that Lacey wasn't going anywhere. It concerned me, because I didn't want Stefan to return Loren to The Brittany Foundation should she and Lacey decide they didn't like each other.

Stefan brought Loren and Lacey to Day In Their Paws, The Brittany Foundation's annual fundraiser in November where volunteers stay up to 24 hours in a kennel with the dog of their choice. Since Loren was gone, I was bunking with Queenie, a sweet ten-year old pit bull with cropped ears.

Stefan, who catered the event, took a break and walked up to our kennel to chat, letting Queenie kiss him through the wire gate.

"I have to tell you, Stefan, I'm a little worried if you keep Lacey that your first loyalty won't be to Loren," I said.

He looked me straight in the eye. "Michelle, I love Loren so much it borders on inappropriate."

I laughed heartily. Loren was safe forever with Stefan, I could feel it in my heart.

Loren and Lacey became true sisters, napping together, playing together and going for runs with Stefan. Yes, Loren the diva was now an L.A. girl, jogging up to four miles a day and riding shotgun on trips to the Hollywood Hills.

As for me, things were never the same at The Brittany Foundation after Loren left. For a while, there was a bright spot named Jake, a one year old black and white male pit bull mixed with American Bulldog rescued from a foster who had taken on too many dogs.

Jake had become my new project. He was huge, about 80 pounds, but gentle, too, dragging me just a little when walking and sitting on my lap in Project Dogway at the ranch. Jake was adorable, like a massive version of the old RCA dog Nipper. Within a few months of

*Jake & his family*

his arrival at Brittany Foundation, Jake started attracting a lot of attention, at events and online, but like Loren before him, no one had followed through. His fate changed in September 2010, when we brought Jake to a big dog adoption event at a park in Saugus.

Early that morning, a pretty brunette in her late teens practically sprinted towards Jake when she saw him. "You are the cutest dog EVER!" she said, nuzzling his big head. "What's your name?"

That was that. Jake found a home, a great one with Ashlyn Burgin and her grandmother, and I was back to feeling a bit lost. It wasn't that I didn't love the remaining dogs at Brittany Foundation, because I did. They just didn't grasp my heart like Loren, then Jake. Perhaps it really is impossible to get over your first love or loves, in my case.

Or maybe I was just getting burnt out. In addition to The Brittany Foundation and Bow-Wows & Meows, a non-profit that adopted out L.A. County shelter pets at an annual pet fair, I'd found myself getting caught up in new scenarios. Raising funds for emergency rescue or medical situations, transporting dogs to their new homes, picking up low-cost dog food and donating it to rescues and pet owners in need, networking shelter or in-danger dogs on Facebook and trying to convince pet owners not to turn their dog into the shelter by providing resources or information. It never ended.

My favorite call came when Nancy from The Brittany Foundation was at the hospital recovering from hip replacement surgery. I was in charge of responding to messages in her absence.

I took a deep breath and exhaled before I called back, conjuring up the diplomatic yet firm persona I'd created to deal with these types of situations.

"Hello," a male voice answered.

"Hi, this is Michelle from The Brittany Foundation returning your call," I said politely.

"Oh hi," he said. "Thanks for calling me back."

"Sure. What can I help you with?"

"Well, we have a female 14-year old Rottie mix that we need to find rescue for."

"Really? Why can't you keep her?"

"We're moving to New Jersey in a few weeks and she's an outside dog." (This was getting better by the minute). "It's too cold out there."

"Well, you could bring her inside. Try crate training her."

"She's not used to that and our landlord doesn't allow pets."

"OK, well, you could try finding a pet-friendly apartment or house," I suggested.

"We already signed a lease," came the exasperated reply.

"You could break the lease. Take your dog with you," I said, very calmly.

"That's not possible," he said, anger growing in his voice. "I'm so sick of you rescues giving me the guilt trip."

"Well, sir," I replied, trying to tamp down my own mounting fury. "You have to understand something. We get calls like this every day. Most, if not all rescues are overcrowded, underfunded and under-staffed. Yet people expect us to take their dogs, every one that crosses our path, and give them a home for the rest of their life if they don't get adopted. We'd love to do that, but it's not always possible."

A big sigh on his end. "Well, we're going to have to take her to the shelter if we can't find a rescue."

I exhaled right back. "Can I tell you something? If you take a 14-year old dog to a shelter, 95 percent or higher chance she will be killed. Plus, she will suffer for three terrifying days before being killed by a stranger. You'd be better off to take her to your vet and have her humanely put down with people she loves surrounding her."

"I really don't want to do that."

"Look, the best help I can offer is for you to send me a photo and bio with contact info so I can post your dog on Facebook. It's a long shot, but you never know. Someone may see her and be able to save your dog," I said. "The cuter the photo, the better."

He did as I asked and I posted his dog on Facebook. About a month later I saw her photo and followed the thread. To my great surprise and delight, she had been rescued by a kind person willing to let an old dog live out the rest of her days in their Southern California backyard.

Still, I knew this was a rarity. Most dogs like that didn't luck out. They ended up in freezer barrels and body bags at your local shelter. The Pandora's Box of animal welfare was opening wider and wider and with it, my anger towards people. Every face I saw at the shelter, online, at The Brittany Foundation, was a direct reflection of human irresponsibility. It consumed my thoughts and my spirit.

Sometimes, depending on my mood and hormonal cycle, all it took was a shelter "RIP" dog photo on Facebook to make me burst into tears. Wayde would see this and ask, "Why are you crying? Don't you know how sad this all is by now?" and I'd reply, "Well, someone has to cry for this dog. Someone has to care."

I continued to make the trek to The Brittany Foundation about once a month, cleaning kennels and spending time with the four-legged residents. Several new volunteers had joined the big dog ranks, including one particularly passionate young woman named Vanessa Visket. She lived in Acton, just a few miles away from The Brittany Foundation, and came every Saturday. Vanessa had fallen for Queenie. She even gave Queenie massages, so the feeling was very mutual.

Tommy Tucker, another double digit resident was claimed by Tiffany Martinez-Wright. Charlie, our charming 70-lb terrier mix who looked like a Jack Russell on steroids, found an advocate in Gwen Romani. Brittany's big dogs were in very good hands

Since I was getting ready to hit the road again to promote "Pit Stops," I needed a canine companion to act as my book tour ambassador and keep me company across all those long, lonely miles. A bomb-proof pit that liked other dogs and would deal well with crowds. While one Brittany dog named Dana, a black and white pit bull, could possibly fit the bill, I decided not to tear her away from her kennel mate Hannah, who would miss her terribly.

Plus, I felt I'd already told the Brittany Foundation's story with Loren. It would be nice to showcase another aspect of rescue. I could spring a shelter pit and try to find it a home along the way, but what if that didn't happen? Brittany Foundation was full and every rescue I knew of was overflowing, as well. I knew I couldn't adopt another dog, so taking a shelter dog would be very irresponsible of me without a rescue lined up.

Maybe I could find a pit bull in foster care, one that was looking for a home, but would have a place to come back to when we returned. A sweetheart that liked other dogs and would charm every human it came across. I had acquired thousands of rescue friends on Facebook, so it couldn't be that hard. It was just a matter of filtering through the hundreds of canine faces and stories I saw streaming by every day.

***

Little Booker was a looker, a brown and white spotted pit bull puppy with an adorable face. He was saved from the streets of the Antelope Valley, where he was being used as a football by some punk kids, by a rescuer who had the courage to step in. Problem was, Booker's savior couldn't keep him. The lucky puppy landed at the Canyon Country home of pet sitter and foster mom extraordinaire Kyle Harris.

Kyle, a Castaic Shelter volunteer, was a friend of mine on Facebook. She had bought a copy of "Pit Stops," but we had never met. Seeing Booker gave me an idea. I had just been assigned to start writing a bi-weekly pet page for The Signal, where I was now working full-time again as assistant features editor, and wanted the first story to be about fostering. Kyle and Booker were perfect.

The Harris home had been remodeled by the television show "Garage Mahal" the year before. What was once a maze of crates and supplies in an overstuffed garage was now a high-end, fully functional kennel indoor/outdoor kennel with a soft bed and plenty of space for Booker. It was a nice set up and Booker seemed very happy to be there.

During the interview, he bounced around the backyard, the vision of cuteness playing with Kyle's own dogs, a mix of rescued Yorkies, terriers and Chihuahuas. Kyle had been fostering Castaic Shelter dogs for years, mostly mamas, puppies or both. Booker was her first pit bull, but Kyle already knew the score.

"There's not a mean bone in his body. Booker's a strong pup; he just needs someone who will continue to train him and not let him jump all over people," she said in the article. "Booker's a great dog. He's going to be a real ambassador for his breed."

It seemed I had a book tour contender. While it might be a challenge to take a puppy across country, a very strong one at that, who could resist Booker's charms?

Not Carol Rock, it seemed. Carol, a Facebook friend and fellow writer in Canyon Country, had seen my post on Booker. She had talked to her husband about considering the puppy as a companion for their older dog. The meet and greet turned into an on-the-spot adoption.

My heart, while joyful for Booker, was also a little heavy. Who would I bring on the road now?

The answer came in January when a new face popped up on Kyle's

*Kara*

Facebook page, an adorable little fawn bully girl with the cutest wrinkled brow, pointy ears and inquisitive gold eyes. Her name was Kara and according to Kyle's post, she was a stellar bully breed: dog-friendly, human adoring and altogether charming.

I had to meet her.

\*\*\*

Our first date went very well, especially since Kara, like any good pit bull, was not shy upon introduction. We were making out in seconds.

Kyle had instructed me to let myself into the backyard, where the outdoor half of Kara's kennel was, since she had some dog sitting engagements.

"You think she'll be OK with me, even though we've never met?" I asked Kyle.

"Kara loves everyone, Michelle. You'll see."

There was no barking as I opened the gate. Kara looked out from the dog door and cocked her head as I approached.

"Hey pretty girl," I said in my sweetest voice, making sure the gate clicked behind me. Kara immediately ran over and grasped my legs in a bear hug. I bent down and patted her head. Kara responded with the first of many licks, almost knocking me over in her exuberance.

Upon closer inspection, I saw that Kara's tail had been cut off very close to the vertebrae, leaving a barely covered nub that furiously moved side to side when she was excited. I sighed and hugged her closer. It wasn't enough for this poor dog to be bred constantly, her body parts had to be crudely hacked off. At least her ears were intact and they were spectacular, crinkly triangles perched on her head like little radars.

"Some attack dog you are," I said, laughing and standing up. "Wanna go for a drive?"

The one possible strike against Kara as my "Pit Stops" companion was that she had a lot of trouble getting in and out of the car, Kyle had told me, and didn't seem to love driving too much. If Kara could become cool with riding shotgun, then Kyle was willing to let her go for a six-week book tour. Today would be the first test.

I went inside the garage to find her leash. Kara ran into her kennel and flung herself on the chain link fencing, still wiggling madly. Leash found, I opened the door and she ran into my arms again, this time splaying her legs across my bended knees for closer contact. I wobbled a bit, but ultimately managed to get the leash on the ebullient Kara.

We walked out to my car, a shiny new black Toyota RAV4. The Tacoma that took Loren and me across country was retired to the dealership with 250,000 miles, still running strong but requiring increasingly more expensive repairs. Wayde was adamant that I get a new car before my newest journey and it made sense, even if the new car payments were painful. Saying goodbye to the Tacoma was hard with all the memories it contained, but I looked forward to making new ones in the RAV4.

I opened the door for Kara and she looked at me blankly, not budging. Patting the seat did not help. She seemed genuinely perplexed. I took her short little arms and put them on the running board. Kara stood splayed there, just about paralyzed, so I continued to lift her rear end, until I was basically picking her up altogether. She was small but dense, probably about 50 pounds.

Kara patiently waited until I got into my seat, sitting up at full attention. I started the engine and her eyes grew wider.

"It's OK, girl," I said softly as I patted Kara's booty. "I'm a good driver. Some people, like my boyfriend, might tell you differently, but I really am."

The RAV4 smoothly moved forward. For the first few minutes, Kara looked intently out of the window, panting. Then she did a little twirl, curled up and laid down. Her breathing became steady and she no longer seemed anxious.

After a few minutes on the street, we hit the highway. As the miles passed, Kara grew sleepy, her eyes closing, placing her heavy yet soft head on my right forearm, which was resting on the console. She gave a sigh and peeked up at me, her forehead wrinkled, before going back to sleep. I stroked her velvet head and smiled, a sense of hope and relief filling my spirit. The search was over.

"You're gonna do just fine, Kara," I told her. "Hope you're up for a road trip."

# Rolling Stones

The landscape was familiar, but my new passenger wasn't yet. Kara and I hurtled along Interstate 15, a long, dry, desolate desert that runs through Las Vegas, for what seemed like eternity. Our goal was to get to St. George, Utah, before nightfall. Kara was sleeping and I was what I liked to call wired and tired, the odd state of not having enough sleep and being completely amped on caffeine at the same time.

I picked Kara up that Monday morning at 10 a.m., a little later than I had hoped, but I had to stop for a breakfast burrito at Telly's Drive Inn in Castaic on the way. Stuffed full of crispy, piping hot potatoes, melted cheese, eggs, guacamole and salsa, it was the best breakfast burrito around and would keep me full until dinner.

*"Let's hit the road!"*

Kara's Angels were gathered at Kyle's house for the big sendoff, including Carol of Lancaster Shelter, along with her friend and fellow volunteer Bonnie Witten. Denise Martin and Clare Storey of Castaic Shelter also met us, as well as my dear friend Yvonne Allbee of Bow-Wows & Meows.

Kara was her usual excitable self amidst the commotion, wiggling her tail-less butt at record speed as everyone kissed her goodbye and sent us off with best wishes. Kyle handed me a bulging, cotton paw-print bag.

"There's different bandannas in here, plus some toys and treats," Kyle said, rustling through the bag before handing me something. "And the book of Kara."

The green plastic binder had a photo of Kara on front, with tips for feeding, what she liked (affection, treats and most of all, a game of fetch), what she was afraid of (wind) and even what her name meant: friend. How appropriate.

"Thanks, Kyle," I said, hugging her close. "I'll take good care of the Chunk." It was Kyle's nickname for Kara, which I loved. I knew she'd have a few more from her Aunt Michelle by the end of the trip.

"I know you will," Kyle said. When we pulled apart, she wiped her eyes. "Maybe we'll even find her a great home."

"I'll do my best."

Kara and I finally hit the road about 11 a.m. For the first 20 minutes, Kara was literally at the edge of her seat, watching the goings on with intense curiosity. She finally settled down, twirling around and making herself comfortable on top of the fuzzy pink blanket Kyle sent along - which was embroidered with blocks that spelled out "I Love My Mommy." Hmm.

Little snores started emitting from Kara, along with a few deep sighs. Something else was being released, too. Like her Pit Stops predecessor, Kara had awful gas. What is it with bullies, anyway? They are the tootiest dogs around. I hadn't even given Kara any human treats yet. This was just her natural state. Whew.

My phone rang, breaking up the monotony.

"Hello," I answered.

"Michelle? Hi, this is Ben Swan from the Santa Fe New Mexican. I got your press release and wanted to ask you a few questions about your book and the signing at Santa Fe Humane Society."

"Great, you caught me at the perfect time. We're just driving across the desert." My heart started to race. It was always strange for me to be interviewed, to be on the other side of the story. I always hoped to do the dogs justice, to present the facts and not say anything stupid that would do them further harm.

"So, how did you get started with all this? Do you have any pit bulls of your own?" Ben asked me.

The question threw me off track. This was tough, determining the most important information to relay. I launched into my story about finding Sam, an American Bulldog/pit mix on Christmas Day 2000. How he had followed me and my pack of black labs and a border collie into a wash where we took our morning walk. He was bitten up, skinny, wearing only a tattered red harness. Sam had taken off as we neared my home, only to reappear on my porch that night.

"Christmas night, stray dog, what are you going to do? I let him in and he never left."

Ben laughed. He sounded young and sharp, yet compassionate. I hoped he wouldn't go for the sensational angle, like so many reporters did when it came to covering pit bulls.

I went on to tell Ben about finding my youngest dog, Buster, as a puppy in a shopping mall parking lot. The little brown, slightly brindle dog ran to everyone's side, as if to say, "Are you my person?" He had one ear sticking up and was as cute as could be. If he were there after I finished with my story, I told myself, I would take him back to The Signal and find him a home. He ended up at mine, of course, since no one else wanted him. We called Buster "The Pog" (part pig, part dog) because of his portly stature and the way he snorted and trotted around like a little truffle pig.

"I'm probably giving you way too much info, huh?" I asked.

"No, you're fine," I could hear Ben's fingers clicking away at the keyboard, a very familiar noise.

As we got further into the interview, I started divulging my feelings about animal welfare, how hard it was dealing with a biased and uneducated public, about shelter workers and volunteers who were often blamed, wrongly in my opinion, for the horrors that occurred there. My stream of consciousness went on for several minutes and all the while, I could hear Ben typing away.

Oh my God, I was one of those rambling subjects, the type I outwardly indulged but inwardly laughed at when I was in reporter mode. As a features writer, I never went for the sensational aspect and would avoid trying to make anyone look foolish, but I wasn't sure how other journalists felt, especially news reporters. I was comfortable talking to Ben and this was dangerous.

"I hope you don't misquote me," I told Ben. The clacking stopped.

"How can I misquote you by what you're saying?" he said, slightly amused.

"Well, I just hope you don't misinterpret my quotes," I said. "Does that make sense? Sometimes in animal welfare, we can get a little passionate and end up looking…crazy. That's not my goal."

"Don't worry," Ben assured me. "I think I understand where you're coming from."

I sighed. "Thank you."

"I'll be there at the Humane Society event. I look forward to meeting you."

"Me, too."

Other than my conversation with Ben, the drive to St. George was uneventful, a bland stretch of highway until we entered the gorgeous red rock landscape of southern Utah.

Kara was a serious napper, like the little kid you put in the car to get to go to sleep. It was only when we came to a stop or would hit one of those highway road grates that Kara arose from the slumber, ears on high alert.

We checked into our room and Kara, who wouldn't jump into the car, managed to hurl herself onto the bed with ease. She blended into the southwestern colors of the room and we both fell asleep about 9 p.m., after I consumed some Thai noodle and tofu takeout.

I had stopped eating meat. It had been on my mind for a while, the hypocrisy of saving dogs while I eat chickens and turkeys or pigs and cows. A visit to The Gentle Barn

*"I could get used to this!"*

in Canyon Country sealed the deal. Ellie, the founder, had given me a tour of the farm animal sanctuary months earlier as I was writing a story for The Signal.

Now, when I thought of chicken, it was "I'm eating Mario," a beautiful black chicken at The Gentle Barn. All turkey had become Monty, their irrepressibly proud Tom with the huge chest that gobbled when you call his name. Once you place a face to the meat in front of you, it greatly loses its appeal.

Giving up beef and pork wasn't a big deal, I hadn't really eaten either consistently for the last year. I still ate seafood on occasion. Yes, I realize fish have feelings, too, but for some reason, it hasn't hit me as hard. Yet. The only time I ate chicken or any other kind of meat was for a restaurant review. I'd take a bite or two and bring the rest back for some hungry reporter in the office.

Honestly, veganism is the only truly ethical diet, because of the horrors of the dairy industry, which I won't get into. Let's just suffice to say that cow's milk comes from pregnant cows. Where do you think the calves end up? For that reason, I have switched to almond milk. It's still too hard for me to imagine a world without cheese and butter, so that step would be a challenge, but something I'm open to down the line.

On our way to the restaurant, two young men asked me if Kara was a bully breed of some kind. When I said yes, they pulled out a little brindle puppy they had just "got." She was adorable, of course. I kissed the little furball on the head and inhaled. There's nothing like that puppy smell. Better than a new car.

The young men walked away and got into their car. I suddenly screamed out, "Don't breed her!" They looked at me, startled, and sped off. I thought briefly about being embarrassed, but then realized one of the blessings of being 42 was that I no longer cared what people thought about me.

That night, I discovered Kara loved sleeping on the bed, nesting into the covers and trying to lie on top of my head like a 50 pound cat. When I pushed her off with a soft "no," she decided to kiss me. And kiss me. And kiss me. Now I like bully kisses as much as the next girl, but even I had my limit.

"No, Kara," I said, to no avail. "Stop!" The sternness in my voice gave way to giggles. I couldn't stay mad at her, but enough was enough. Finally, I put a pillow in front of my face, only to have Kara's paws tunnel through, then her face, then her tongue.

I turned over to the other side. Kara finally took the hint and found her way to my feet, hugging my legs as she slowly fell asleep, her soft snores punctuating the silence.

***

Our drive to Kanab the next morning was an easy 90 miles, so we slept in and grabbed a veggie breakfast sandwich at Starbucks before heading out.

The scenic route led through the idyllic towns of Rockville and Springdale on the way to Zion National Park, a community chock full of bed and breakfasts, restaurants, art galleries and orchards. The setting was so tranquil even the horses were asleep in pastures as we drove by.

Watching those majestic mountains arise in the distance always took my breath away, even though I've been through Zion three times before. It was simply magnificent, the layers of burgundy, orange, green and gold, jutting out into the universe sharply or unfolding in a valley of stunning stone. I always wonder what our ancestors must have thought the first time they saw it. Probably the same thing everyone else does – Mother Nature does some amazing work.

The park ranger at Zion directed us to Pa'Rus, the one dog-friendly trail in all of Zion. It was paved and flat, accessible enough that a woman on her scooter had no problem cruising along. Kara had a blast, sniffing about the trail at a rapid pace. She didn't look athletic,

*"Is that a squirrel?"*

with her barrel body and stumpy legs, but Kara can keep up with the best of them.

The scenery was gorgeous, rushing rivers running through all that glorious stone, the sun bright, the sky clear. We walked about 2.5 miles round trip, a welcome stretch of movement after being cooped up in the car. Kara attracted many admirers along the way, but not everyone became a fan.

On our trek back, I watched a man as he spotted us, curling the leash to his fluffy shepherd mix tightly around his hand. "She's friendly," I called out, but he was focused straight ahead. Meanwhile, a Jack Russell saw Kara and immediately started barking. Kara cocked her head and stared, but didn't bark back.

"The smallest ones have the biggest attitude, huh, Kara?" I said and stroked her back.

In the dark, mile-long tunnel heading out of Zion, I honked like the dork that I am (no one else did) and marveled at the bits of beauty peeking through the small, carved windows before we emerged into yet another spectacular mountainous sight. The landscape in Zion and Southern Utah in general is eerie, like another planet, with its layers of stone in every shape and color, from the sharpest sphere to round rocks coiled up like cinnamon rolls.

We checked into the Quail Park Lodge in Kanab, home of Best Friends Animal Society, and took a luxurious hour-long nap. I had a book signing scheduled at the Rocking V, the hippest restaurant in town, but the weather was not cooperating. It was rainy and cold, not ideal for an outdoor event, so I decided to keep Kara in the car and move it inside.

Ed Fritz, who wrote the foreword to "Pit Stops," met me for dinner...and he was the only one. The signing was a flop. I had brought 500 books with us for the tour and was disheartened by our first event. Hopefully, it wasn't an ominous sign for the rest of the trip.

On the positive side, I had a very nice birthday meal with Ed, who had done wonders for bully breeds as the Best Friends campaign specialist for Pit Bulls: Saving America's Dog.

Ed had traveled all over the country to prevent breed specific legislation from passing with attorney Ledy VanKavage, the campaign's director. The duo was successful more than 90 percent of the time, a very impressive track record.

We tucked into a tasty trio of rustic hummus with homemade flat bread and caught up. Ed was in the midst of a transition, since the campaign's grant no longer covered his position. He was considering a move to Southern California to become the executive director of a German Shepherd rescue.

"Do you really think there will be a day where there's no more homeless pets?" I asked.

"I think it's possible, but it's a challenge," he said. "What about you?"

"No, I don't. I think the public is too irresponsible. I think it'll get better, that we'll get close, but you're never going to fix the 10 percent of idiots who won't do the right thing."

"Such a pessimist."

"I know, right? I used to be a Pollyanna, but after all I saw on the first trip, I just can't believe that human nature is going to change to the extent it would take to make that happen."

"I'm a little more optimistic, but it's not going to be easy."

Our order came. Ed had chosen a meat dish, while I had the couscous cakes with a zesty basil sauce. Crisp yet succulent, the cakes were very satisfying and I felt great sticking to my vegetarian goal.

"What do you think of the no-kill movement?" I asked Ed between bites. "Do you think it's possible?"

"Well, it's kind of disingenuous to call a no-kill shelter no-kill, because they pick and choose what animals come in," Ed replied.

"Exactly. Everyone loves to tout no-kill, but how do you accomplish that when supply outstrips demand? Is there any open door shelter that is truly no-kill?"

"It's really rare, but there's Nevada Humane Society. They do amazing work."

I smiled. "Cool, Kara and I are going there. It's our last stop on the trip."

After sharing a stellar crème brulee for dessert, Ed came to the car to meet Kara. She jumped out of the passenger side and right into his arms.

"Oh, she's an awesome travel buddy, huh?" Ed said, kissing and hugging Kara, who reciprocated tenfold.

"She sure is," I said proudly.

## Rolling Stones

\*\*\*

After a solid night's sleep, Kara and I departed for our long trip to Moab, Utah. We were connecting with my friend Courtney and her two year old son Elijah. Courtney and I had met when I did a story on pilates for The Signal about eight years ago. She briefly moved to Pine Mountain Club and we became fast friends.

When my black lab Rudy died of a seizure at 6 a.m. on a Sunday morning, Courtney was the person who helped me move his 90 pound body out of my two story cabin, dried my tears and drove us to the vet, in the snow, so I could have him cremated. That kind of character was hard to find. I missed Courtney tremendously after she moved back to Salt Lake City.

We had reserved a small cabin outside at an RV resort of Arches National Park, one of the most gorgeous spots in the country, if the photos were any indication. Our route was Highway 12, which is a scenic byway for good reason. It's an endless display of Mother Nature's finest work. During the four hour drive, we encountered everything from natural, red rock archways to the Escalante Staircase, an infinite vista of colorful rock formations to snow. Yes, snow in May. Thankfully, the RAV had all wheel drive.

Kara and I stopped for lunch at the Burr Trail Grill along the way. Inside the vibe was very rustic, crunchy even, with earthy young waitresses and a menu featuring local beef raised just outside the restaurant's doors. I opted for the Madras sandwich, an excellent combination of grilled veggies with a flavorful onion marmalade atop a grilled, yet still soft focaccia roll along with herbed new potatoes. On the counter were cookies the size of hubcaps and in a pastry case, fruit and cream pies. Decisions, decisions. A slice of boysenberry pear pie was the winner.

I took the food back to my car, where Kara watched with mild interest as I devoured my lunch. It was 2 p.m. and I was starving. Kara's gold eyes bore into mine, her head on the console. Guilty, I dug out a snack from the bag Kyle had packed. She chomped it down happily and sighed, her eyes closing in satisfaction.

The second half of our journey was a little scary. As the elevation rose, so did the snow levels. At first, it was just a few patches on the hillsides, then little flakes began to appear. I slowed down, though I

Pit Stops 2

was concerned we weren't going to make it in time to meet Courtney. The last thing I wanted was an accident, to plunge off those beautiful mountains into a ditch, putting Kara in harm's way or ruining my new RAV4. Nope, better to take it easy and take in the scenery.

Finally, the twists and turns ended and merged into a long, smooth highway, which suited Kara much better. She didn't like the winding roads, often popping up and swaying back and forth, then putting her head on my arm for reassurance. Driving with the equivalent of a bowling ball weighing on my free arm wasn't working.

I'd try to put Kara back in her seat, but she was one determined dog. Soon enough, Kara's big old noggin would be right back on me, her eyes closed, trying to make the best out of a wild ride.

*"Are we there yet?"*

We arrived at Archview Campgrounds about 5:30 p.m., earlier than I anticipated. It was a very welcoming spot, decked out in old Western décor, with a well-stocked grocery store, picnic areas, a playground and a couple of teepees. Better yet, there was a wide open, fenced-in area that was "closed for day use." Perfect.

I asked the manager if I could play ball with Kara there and she agreed. Courtney and Elijah had arrived, so we all made our way over, Elijah pushing his little plastic lawn mower and Kara growing more excited by the second once I whipped out her red ball. Her eyes never left my hand until I threw it across the dusty lot.

Watching Kara fetch was a joy. She charged after the ball, running full force and skidding or grinding to a halt in the red dirt while I laughed at her antics. We did this for 20 minutes before wandering over to the horse area, where Courtney and Elijah had moved to. Panting, Kara assumed her favorite position in front of the horses. Her front legs would go stock straight, while her back legs splayed behind her, and those ears would point to the heavens. I called it the platypus.

"Wow," Kara seemed to think as she surveyed the scene. "Those are awful big dogs!" The horses just silently stared at her and she quietly returned their gaze, totally Zen.

Back at our basic cabin, a tiny space equipped with two bunk beds, a mini fridge, a porch and cooking area with grill and picnic table, Courtney started preparing us dinner. We sat outside and she grilled tequila lime salmon burgers from Whole Foods, on top of toasted baguette with lemon aioli and spring mix.

*"Whoa, Nelly!"*

"You're the best, Courtney," I grinned.

She hugged me in response. Courtney gave the best hugs, strong, heartfelt embraces from the core of her being.

Following dinner, Elijah scooted his way through the campgrounds on his plastic motorcycle while Kara and I ambled along his side. A man spotted Kara and walked on over. "I just have to ask, what kind of dog is she?" he said.

"She's a pit bull or bully breed of some kind. She came from the shelter."

"Well, she's certainly unique. I've never seen another dog like her," he said, patting Kara's head with affection.

"She's one of a kind," I said with a sigh. I was falling in love with the Chunk. It was hard not to.

\*\*\*

Like rolling stones, we were calling wherever we lay our heads our home. A mattress pulled from the top bunk onto the floor served as our bed the first night in Moab. Kara conked out and slept for nine hours straight, her little legs outstretched in front of her. She only kissed me for a few minutes before assuming this position, which allowed me to get a good night's sleep, too.

In the morning, Courtney, Elijah and I busied ourselves with breakfast and getting ready for a trip into town and Arches National Park. Kara just watched the action intently from her perch on the mattress. She was extremely gentle with Elijah, not reacting to his sometimes unpredictable movements or when he pushed his toys around the small cabin.

It helped that she had played fetch for a good half hour before breakfast. We awoke early, as the sun was just starting to rise. In that dusty lot, Kara chased the ball around like an agility champ, catching it in mid-air at times. This caused me to silently raise my arms in a "V." I didn't want to wake up anyone camping nearby with our antics.

The ball quickly became caked with mud, but that didn't stop Kara. Her gold green eyes would fixate on that dirty thing until I threw it again, and again, and again. Finally, she was panting and drooling enough to call it quits. Still, Kara never let that filthy ball out of her sight all the way back to camp.

We had made some friends in camp, two older gentlemen riding quads that took a liking to Elijah. They offered to take Elijah, who was fascinated with their vehicles, for a ride around the campgrounds. Then they said Courtney could take him herself, if she'd like. Courtney hopped on the quad, put a delighted Elijah in front of her and slowly cruised around for 10 minutes. Both of them were giddy when they circled our cabin. Spencer and Gary, the quad owners, really made their day.

After stopping for provisions at a store in downtown Moab, which was bustling with bicyclists, motorcycles, climbers, white water rafters and tour buses, we stopped for lunch at Palente's Deli, where I had a fantastic Mediterranean veggie sandwich stuffed with homemade hummus, soft crumbles of feta and marinated eggplant, peppers and onions on toasty fresh harvest wheat bread. Delish.

The weather was perfect for sightseeing: blue sky, scattered clouds, temps in the low 70s. We paid our $10 fee at Arches National Park and took a leisurely drive through the many spectacular rock formations on display. No dogs were allowed on the trails, so we'd pull over and surreptitiously take photos at standout locations, such as The Organ, an immensely tall tower that looked as though it had been chiseled by a talented, giant artist. We walked a little further and saw a blanket of green in the valley below, stunning against the red rocks.

Across the way, what looked like three stone woman chatting up to the heavens, aptly named Three Gossips, literally took my breath away.

*"Hey, Elijah, say cheese!"*

The Acropolis in Greece was cool when my sister and I saw them a few decades ago, but honestly, this landscape is even more stunning, otherworldly in both color and structure.

We went back to camp, for a nap and a shower, before returning to town for Thai takeout, which we ate outside our cabin. This might sound strange, nature and Asian food, but don't knock it until you've tried it. Somehow the spicy drunken noodles, luscious mango shrimp curry and fresh vegetable spring rolls hit just the right spot and there was no clean up afterwards.

On our way to the bathroom, Kara quietly slipped out of her chain and introduced herself to a small black and tan dog and its owners. I panicked at first, but quickly remembered that Kara's gentle soul extends to her four-legged counterparts. She simply sniffed the other dog, who accepted Kara with a wagging tail.

"Sorry about that," I said to the owner, pulling on Kara's collar and putting the chain back around her neck.

"No problem," the woman said. "What kind of dog is she?"

"She's a bully breed. I wrote a book about pit bulls and Kara's my pit bull ambassador."

"Oh, that's great. Where did she come from?"

"The shelter. She was pregnant, and when her puppies got adopted, Kara was going to be killed, until a foster took her in. She's looking for a home."

The couple nodded. "We rescued Roxy from the Humane Society in Florida," the man said. "They had taken in a bunch of dogs from the Bahamas, after a hurricane."

"Feral dogs feed off of the crust from pots there," the woman said. "They call them pot cakes."

"Wow, you learn something never every day. Bless you for saving her."

They smiled and moved on. Kindred spirits were everywhere.

\*\*\*

The next morning, after yet another energetic game of catch, Kara and I bid Courtney and Elijah goodbye. First, we took some photos in the camp's teepees, which Kara was none too fond of. She hopped right out when I tried to snap a shot of her alone.

Our drive to Santa Fe was long, close to 400 miles. There were some pretty national monuments to look at along the way, for the first 100 miles or so, then it turned into barren, neutral desert. Our La Quinta room was very welcoming, with a king-sized bed that had

Kara's name all over it. She hopped right up and twirled around to nest herself in the mountain of pillows.

"You're too much, Chunkarella," I said, patting her affectionately. It was one of several nicknames I had come up with for Kara, including Sweet Pea and Kare Bear.

The hotel clerk recommended Horseman's Haven for an authentic Southwestern dinner. It was right across the street. I ordered the blue corn cheese enchiladas and a small side of guacamole, with chips and salsa, for which they charged me an extra $7. What are you going to say in a situation like that, though? Um, I think you're an extortionist? Usually, I give a tip on takeout, but not that time.

Upon opening the Styrofoam container, I was disappointed. The meal was a gloppy, harshly spicy mess of beans, rice, sauce and cheese, one barely distinguishable from the other. I ate about one-third of it before giving up and turning to the chips and guacamole, which were quite tasty.

Searching online, I found Ben Swan's story on us in the Santa Fe New Mexican. I needn't have worried. He did a great job. Hopefully it would bring out a crowd for our second signing.

The shelter was about five miles away from our hotel, in a rural location. A long dirt road led to two newer Adobe style buildings, one for animal intake, the other a dedicated adoption center, both built in 2005. The impressive lobby featured high-beamed ceilings, rustic tile floors and windows that allowed visitors to view the cat adoption area.

Kara was greeted by a cache of enthusiastic volunteers. She responded by flopping on the ground and rolling over.

"What a chunk!" one volunteer exclaimed, rubbing her belly.

*"Sure, you can call me Chunk!"*

# Pit Stops 2

*"Ben is my friend!"*

"That's so funny. That's her nickname!"

Another came up and kissed Kara on top of the head. "What a sweet pea."

I laughed. "I call her that, too. She's the sweetest pea."

Ben came to meet us shortly after the signing started. He was about my age, outfitted in a dapper hat and snappy sport coat. In addition to writing for the paper, Ben was also the special projects manager for the shelter, including their cool thrift store in town called Look What the Cat Dragged In.

He and his partner Ricky, an adoption counselor at the shelter, owned four dogs, including a pit mix, and fostered, too. I inwardly groaned for envisioning Ben as a rookie reporter that might not understand rescue.

He sat on the leather bench and pulled Kara onto his lap, rubbing her belly and hugging her tight. I liked Ben as much as Kara did.

The SFHS was running a pit bull special that weekend, in conjunction with the signing, with adoption fees half off for pit bulls over six months old. "We also offer free training with pit bull adoptions," Ben said. "We really push that."

While SFHS, which is an open door shelter, had an impressive 82-89 percent live release rate, bully breeds are often the last to be adopted.

"They start out well in here, they're happy, but the longer they stay, the more they deteriorate," Ben said. "We try to foster them out, to give them a break, or if we can't save them for whatever reason, we work with other rescues in different areas, where they might have more success in getting adopted."

SFHS had recently hired a certified pet trainer to evaluate dogs and create an appropriate training regimen. A humane walking program had also been put in place.

"Our dogs get out two to three times a day. They learn to eliminate while they're on a leash, which makes them more adoptable," Ben said. "Oftentimes, people will bring a dog back to us if they can't be housebroken."

Ben gave Kara and me a brief tour of the shelter, which had huge fenced-in play yards for the dogs to run around or socialize in pairs. Kara trotted happily around the red dirt, scurrying after the tennis ball Ben found and threw for her. It was windy and cool out, perfect for little Kara not to get overheated.

From what I could see, the dogs had large, clean chain link kennels furnished with dog houses and bedding. There were about five pit bulls in the dog population. While SFHS does not do house checks for pit bull adoptions, which many shelters require, potential owners do have to fill out an extensive application.

If there are any red flags, adoption counselors such as Thomas, a kind pony-tailed young man who babysat Kara for a few minutes while I packed up the car following the book signing, have the right to refuse potential adopters.

"You'll see it from the way they fill out an application or just get the feeling that the dogs wouldn't be adopted for the right reasons," Thomas said. "Sometimes I think they'd just be better off here, where they get fed and walked every day, but we can't keep them all. Right now we're completely maxed out on space."

## Back on the Bayou

Driving across Texas is never my favorite thing to do. It seems endless, all that asphalt surrounded by dry brush and vacant buildings. Since I knew what I was getting myself into for those 500 miles from Santa Fe to Wichita Falls, I stopped at Borders and bought "Life" by Keith Richards on CD.

It made for good company, as did Kara, decked out in her new red harness, courtesy of Ben. The choke or pinch collar which Kara had been wearing was not in favor at Santa Fe Humane Society. As a matter of fact, Ben didn't run our picture with his story because Kara was wearing the pinch collar in it. "A lot of people really look down on that," he explained.

I was neutral on the topic. The pinch collar was what Kyle had sent with us, so that's what I used. I don't think it's cruel, even if it might look that way. It's just effective for strong dogs that pull. The harness would work just as well, I imagined from my experience with Loren. Sure enough, Kara quickly adjusted to her snappy red rig lightning quick, walking as well in it as she did on the collar.

When we'd had our signing at SFHS, a woman came up to us and tentatively patted Kara on the head, unlike the pit lovers, who would immediately embrace or kiss her.

"I'm conflicted about pit bulls, I'll admit it," she told me. "There was news of an attack out here recently. A child was killed by a couple of pit bulls."

"That's horrifying," I replied in a steady voice. "Really tragic." I was about to go into my usual line of questioning, what were the circumstances, are you sure they were pit bulls, etc., but she beat me to the punch.

"I know there are reasons these things happen, bad owners and whatever, but still. It doesn't help that they have that locking jaw."

"Actually, they don't have a locking jaw. No dog does. That's a myth. Pit bulls are just very strong dogs and thus, can do more damage than some of the smaller breeds."

"Well, that's good to know. I won't say that they have a locking jaw anymore," the lady said, looking down at Kara, who had a big, drooly grin on her face. "But I'm still conflicted."

"You're allowed to be conflicted. That's your right," I said.

My sister Heidi wasn't sure about pit bulls either, but she did read my blog and supported my fundraising efforts, which I appreciated. Her husband, Andy, however, un-friended me on Facebook for all my pit bull posts. An LAPD sergeant, Andy firmly believed that pit bulls should not be pets, that they were all dangerous, despite the facts I and the rest of the pit bull community would present to him. What can you do? I know pits can be a polarizing topic, but I won't back down in trying to help them.

"Please, just don't condemn the entire breed for the actions of a few dogs," I told the woman. "There are probably reasons that the attack happened, but it still doesn't make it any less sad."

I thought of this conversation as I looked at Kara softly sleeping in the car. Her big noggin bobbed up and down in the passenger seat while we drove along. Eyes half-closed, Kara emitted little grunts or sighs that turned into steady snoring as the miles zoomed past. I found this endlessly endearing and draped my arm around her back.

Hundreds of thousands of Karas, if not millions, are killed at shelters every year. There were five bully breeds at Santa Fe Humane Society that day, none of whom got adopted. Interest, yes. Homes, no. Many pit bulls are not adopted because of perceptions like that woman's. Pit bulls are mean. They're unpredictable. They go crazy in their old age. You can throw statistics around to educate, to combat the sensationalism with facts like pit bulls rate among the top five breeds for temperament. Or that there are five million pit bull type dogs in America and maybe 20-25 dog attacks per year, which is a rather infinitesimal ratio. Add to that, how many of those dogs are really pit bulls? And, if the myth that all pit bulls went crazy as they got older was true, wouldn't there be many, many more reported attacks?

In my experience, pit bulls were the sweetest, funniest, most affectionate dogs around. Kara was no exception, with her little butt that wiggled at a furious pace whenever she got excited (which was often). Since she had no tail, Kara's booty had to work overtime to convey her happiness. I'm not sure why her tail is gone, no one at the shelter knew, either. My jaded mind thinks it was so her former "owners" would have an easier time of breeding Kara. Maybe it was an aesthetic thing. Who knows.

What I do know is that Kara would have been killed, had it not been for the actions of the volunteers at Lancaster Shelter, who saw how sweet she was, and Kyle, who stepped up as a final foster. All these strokes of luck added up to Kara being a passenger on a 50-day road trip as an ambassador for her breed. There were many Karas that were not so fortunate, however. It broke my heart.

A lot of people asked me if I was excited about taking this trip, like I was in 2009. Honestly, the answer was no. The first time around with Loren, I was a passionate yet naïve new advocate on a mission. I truly believed I could, almost singlehandedly, turn the pit bull image around by traveling across country, handing out a few post cards and letting people interact with a sweet pit bull. Then I saw how large, pervasive and complex the problem was from coast to coast and it burst my crusader bubble.

No, this time around I knew what I was getting myself into. I'd accepted that the problems for these animals exist. This was an important key for me, another lesson learned in recovery. Acceptance does not mean approval. You have to accept what you're dealing with first, though, if you're going to make any effort to change it

Still, there was part of me that missed the idealism, the hope, the belief that I could somehow turn the ship around in record time. Yes, I did what I could, but it just felt like such an uphill battle when I knew that four to six million adoptable animals are killed every year. Those statistics made me want to crawl under a blanket and never come out. So, I tried my best not to do that and instead focus on the one dog at a time that I could help. But was that enough?

There were "bigger" problems in the world, I understood. People didn't have jobs. They were losing their homes or cars. It was hard to feed and clothe the kids. But helping homeless pets had a hold of my heart and my head. It drove me and gave me purpose. Why? Because I feel that animals are truly the most innocent of creatures. They absolutely have no voice. Even children, at some point, can tell you they are being harmed or abused. Animals never have that option.

I stroked Kara's Frappucino-colored forehead and thought of the hell she must had gone through in her life. Yet she hopped in a car with me, someone she barely knew, and trusted that I would do right by her. Kara would fix her loving gaze on me and I'd wonder, who could have let this sweetheart run away, or worse, dumped her on the streets, pregnant, to fend for herself? Who does that? As a society, why are these living, loving beings so disposable? Why aren't they looked on as truly part of the family and held onto for dear life?

Sometimes I felt like Sarah Connor in "Terminator 2," where she looks at the schoolyard and sees a nuclear war coming on whereas everyone else just sees happy kids playing. I'm haunted by the holocaust these animals face every day. Not just the pit bulls, but the sweet Labradors and fluffy kitties, too. The pregnant Chihuahuas. The arthritic, graying seniors. All of them. What is wrong with us, as a culture, to let this happen? Why won't we make it stop?

Kara and I took a break at a gas station in Denton, Texas. She slowly awoke from a nap, stretched out, then jumped out of the car. There was a field behind the station, lush with tall green grass. A tractor cut through a field in the distance. The sun was shining. Kara looked at the ball with palpable excitement.

I chucked it as far as I could. She ran through the tall blades, jumped in the air and caught the ball before it landed. I cheered and she ran back, her stumpy legs going full speed before she practically skidded to a stop before me.

"More?" Her gold eyes asked me as she dropped the slobbery ball in the grass.

I threw it again.

*\*\**

If anyone remembers from the first "Pit Stops," I'm really not a camping girl. Sure, if someone else does the work, pitches the tent, makes the food, I'm down. On my own, not so much.

However, I wanted to mix things up on this trip, really get into nature and have a brief absence from the electronics that seem to rule my life. So Kara and I left the sanctity of our Wichita Falls hotel room destined for outdoor adventure at Cypress Black Bayou Recreation Area about 325 miles away.

It looked nice enough. About 15 miles from Shreveport, the surrounding area was lush, almost tropical with brick track homes surrounded by never-ending lawns. The winding road took us to the gate of Black Bayou. I stopped to make a reservation and ask some questions. The first, of course…"Do you have gators in the park?"

"Well, ma'am, we have some on the far north end, not near the camping sites," said the nice clerk, a young, tanned woman with numerous piercings.

In California, I'm offended when people call me ma'am, taking it as reference to my age. In the south, it's just a form of politeness. Or so I tell myself.

"OK," I took a deep breath. "How about snakes?"

"I'm not going to lie. We do have snakes here, especially this time of year. I hate snakes," she said, shaking her shoulders and head about wildly, the universal sign for the heebie jeebies.

"Do they go in the campground?"

"Well, sometimes they do, but if you have a dog, they shouldn't come around," she said, infinitely patient. "We've never had anyone complain of having one in the tent."

*Camping platypus*

I paused for about 15 seconds. Was I going to puss out and go to a hotel or just deal with the elements? How realistic was it to get bit by a snake or eaten by a gator here, anyway? Probably the same as getting hit by lightning. I would not let fear control me, like I did in Florida with Loren.

"Alright," I said. "We'll take a campsite for a few nights."

We scouted the campgrounds, which only had about three other sites occupied, and picked T-11, right near the lake or body of water, the one I was assured was gator-less. It was very picturesque and better yet, an ideal spot to play fetch.

That's the first thing we did, to get Kara good and tired so I could focus on setting up camp, my first time with the new equipment I purchased before the trip. Kara loved being able to skid in the soft grass, sometimes catching the ball in mid-air and coming down on her side, prompting a high-speed roly poly.

Once Kara was tired from all the action (or I should say, after I cut her off, because that dog would go on until she dropped from a heart attack), I took out the lounge chair from the RAV and tied the leash around it. Kara watched with curiosity as I continued to pull the tent, then the air mattress. Her eyes really grew wide when I started to pitch the tent.

OK, so I am just about the least mechanical person around, but tents nowadays are fairly idiot-proof. The poles are strung together and there were only two of them. How hard could it be? The tent went up pretty quick, once I actually read the instructions, an extreme rarity for me. I hate instruction manuals. So boring. I usually try to figure it out myself, but this was only one page.

It was a little confusing, but I managed to erect the tent, which looked pretty textbook, if slightly crooked on one side.

"Yeah!" I told Kara, who was panting off in the shade. It was muggy and warm here. Actually, it was like being in a steam bath, minus the ability to open a door and escape.

The air mattress confounded me and I was not amused upon discovering the included air pump needed batteries (something Coleman failed to mention on the packaging). This prompted a trip into town for a pillow (which I had forgot to bring from home), the aforementioned batteries, ice and some healthy dinner items (Greek and potato salad, a fruit smoothie) to make up for the shrimp po' boy and French fries I'd had for lunch. Hey, when in Rome, right?

Filling the air mattress went smoothly and our camp was beginning to look like home. Our neighbor, a construction worker from Mansfield, Louisiana, introduced himself to us as Robert. He stayed at the camp when he had work in the area, rather than drive 90 minutes each way.

Robert pointed out the other campers. "The guy on the end is kind of belligerent. He and his wife have lived here for nine years."

"Wow. Well, I might be pissy if I had to camp for nine years, too."

"Good point. Hey, you know that show Billy the Exterminator?"

I nodded, intrigued. Wayde and I had watched the show a few times. Basically, it's about a redneck exterminator named Billy, who proudly sports a blonde mullet and hunts wild animals, many of which we'd never heard of before. We laughed at how backwoods it was.

"His business is just a few miles down, right by the Chevron on your way in," Robert said. "One of the raccoons he found on his show lives in the campground zoo now."

Somehow this didn't comfort me. Billy was called upon to "relocate" all sorts of creepy crawlies and gee, he lived right down the road. Great.

Despite this newfound knowledge, and the incessant, deafening quacking of ducks and chirping of crickets, Kara and I slept pretty well our first night at Black Bayou.

Grooming the next morning was not such a successful endeavor. There were bugs galore in the campground bathroom, plus a huge swamp cooler fan as loud as an airplane engine. Visions of being attacked and no one hearing me scream because of that damn fan had me getting in and out of there in record time. Forget the shower. It was only for a few days. Kara wouldn't complain about me smelling less than fresh.

With no plans for the day, I set up the folding chair in front of the lake and threw the ball to Kara in the morning, at lunch and in early evening, entertained by autobiographies of Michelle Phillips, of The Mamas and The Papas, and Dallas Taylor, a drummer from Crosby, Stills, Nash and Young. Both had the familiar crash and burn to redemption themes found in such autobiographies, as did Keith Richard's "Life."

When I'm home, I'm usually working on promoting "Pit Stops" or volunteering or catching up on chores, so to have this time to focus on my first love, reading, was greatly appreciated. My respect for musicians is immense, even though they tend to be disasters in their personal lives. If I could do it all over again, I would probably pick up a guitar when I was young, instead of a book, and try to become a rock star like Joan Jett, who has to be just about the coolest person on the planet or Chrissie Hynde, who's right behind her.

That night, I decided to go to a recovery meeting in Shreveport, held at a women's sober living home. That's the amazing thing about the program, you can drop in anywhere in the country (or world) and instantly feel at home with people who share your experience, strength and hope.

Gratitude came over me. If it wasn't for my sobriety, I wouldn't be in Louisiana with Kara, promoting my book. I would still be on my porch, getting drunk alone after work every night, waiting for the perfect man or the perfect job. My favorite fantasy was that I would be a famous writer someday. Problem was I never actually wrote anything except sad journal entries that I could barely read the next day.

After the meeting, I took Kara for a walk around the block, only up one street, as it looked a little shady: dilapidated houses in need of paint or repair, broken fences, overgrown lawns, rusty cars from the 70's and 80's, and barking dogs.

A huge young man called from across the way. He looked like a live action Fat Albert and he was headed straight towards us. "That's a pretty dog. Is she friendly?"

"Yes. She's very friendly. Her name's Kara. I wrote a book on pit bulls and she's my pit bull ambassador."

The guy raised an eyebrow before bending down to pet Kara. "Where'd you get her? I like her color."

"She's from a shelter in California. I'm sure you could find a dog just like Kara at a shelter around here," I replied.

"How much does that cost?"

"Probably around $100, but she'd be fixed and up to date on shots."

"Oh, I don't want her to be fixed. I'd want to breed her with my male pit."

Oh no. Keep it together, Sathe. "Why would you want to do that? To make money?"

"Yeah, to make money from the puppies."

"Well, you know a lot of times, people breed pit pups and they don't sell. Then they end up at the shelter, where they are killed. Or you sell them and the owners don't want to deal with them when they get big and they end up in a shelter," I said, trying to keep my cadence comprehensible and non-judgmental. "You know there are hundreds of thousands of pit bulls like this in shelters that end up being killed every year, right? Please don't breed your dog."

His watery bloodshot eyes seemed to take in some, if not all of the rapid-fire information I was throwing out. "Yeah, I got my male from the shelter. They were going to kill him. I built him a chain-link enclosure and a wooden fence around that, so no one can see him."

Great. An unfixed male pit bull living in semi-captivity, yet another recipe for success.

"Well, do you exercise him? That's really important."

"I do on weekends, I take him for a long walk."

"Well, that's good, but you should try to walk him every day. It's so important for young, active dogs."

The guy nodded, transfixed on Kara. I wanted to run, but couldn't just yet. I was desperate to penetrate this guy's consciousness.

"Please don't breed your dog. Please," I begged. "I know you probably think I'm crazy, but I see so many of these dogs being killed. It's horrible."

"Ugh, well, alright," he said. "Hey, there's these guys selling Chihuahuas at the store up the road for like $50."

I shook my head in disgust. "Pit bulls and Chihuahuas make up about 80 percent of the dogs at shelters in California. Most of them don't get out alive. It's very sad. I really hope you don't breed your dog."

He finally stood up and parted from Kara. This was our out. "We gotta go. Have a good night," I said, quickly pulling Kara in to the opposite direction.

"You, too."

I let go of the deep breath I'd been holding in and made my way down the street. There was a woman smoking in front of the sober living home and she called out to Kara.

"Pretty girl!"

Of course, Kara took that as an invitation to hug her legs and lean up for a kiss.

"I hope you don't mind. She's very affectionate," I said.

"No problem. I love dogs."

A few more women came over and asked about the trip. A very respectable looking lady with short hair and glasses, probably in her late 40s or 50s, whipped out her cell phone to show off photos of her two pits lounging on the floor.

The male was named Saddlebag, because her husband had found the emaciated, 20-lb, five-month old dog at a gas station and managed to fit him into his motorcycle saddlebag for the drive home.

"We call him Baggers for short. They are just the best dogs around. I'm so glad you're doing this. And I just love this one..." she said, bending down to her knees and letting Kara make out with her.

"Well, I'm glad you rescued your dogs and that you're such a responsible pit bull mama. People need to see that women like us have these dogs. That it's not just the gang-bangers and criminals, ya know?"

"I do," my new friend said, nodding in agreement, looking wistfully at Kara. "I do."

Kara and I drove back to camp in the dark and quickly settled in our makeshift home. It was about 80 degrees out and breezy. A half hour later, that nice breeze turned into major winds that howled and strained our little tent to what I thought might be the breaking point. I watched as the crooked corner bent even further. When the winds would temporarily die, I'd kick it back into place with little success.

Poor Chunk. "The Book of Kara" warned she didn't like the wind. However, my little friend made not a whimper. Her ears perked up and she nuzzled closer to me, but remained silent. I patted her big head and said soothingly, "Don't worry, Kara. We'll be OK. You're such a good girl..."

Meanwhile, I imagined our tent taking off into the stratosphere like Dorothy's house in "Wizard of Oz," but I kept up the calm exterior. Realistically, I reasoned to myself, our couple hundred pounds of body weight and equipment should keep us anchored. We would be OK.

The winds went on for hours. The only blessing is that it shut up the damn ducks that had relentlessly quacked throughout the night before. Occasionally, I'd hear Kara softly snoring and start to drift off, too, reminding myself that tomorrow we'd have a real roof over our heads.

In the morning, still fuzzy from lack of sleep, I saw a small, dark snake wriggle in the grass as I folded up the tarp. Thankfully, Kara was already in the car. I let out a horror-movie worthy scream and ran away from it. No one came to my rescue.

***

It was strange revisiting many of the places Loren and I had been. In Louisiana, we stopped at the same visitor center sign. In Lafayette, we stayed at the same hotel. Kara walked the same path Loren did as she took her potty breaks. That's where the similarities ended with the two. While both are infinitely sweet, they were quite different dogs.

Loren would endlessly pose for photos, a canine supermodel. She adapted to every situation on our trip beautifully, as if born to travel, turning on the charm with everyone she met. Loren had a limit to her cuddliness, though. After a while a switch would go off, and like Garbo, she'd want to be alone. Loren would stubbornly cross her paws when she didn't want to go somewhere and was somewhat picky about her food but I was cool with that. She deserved to be a diva sometimes after spending so much time in a kennel.

With Kara, the affection never stopped, whether we were in an air-conditioned motel room or outside in the most humid weather. There were no food issues with Kara, she'd gratefully eat everything put in front of her. She didn't pose well for photos, though, being too intent on trying to kiss you and of course, if you had a ball or Frisbee in your hand, forget it. Unlike her sophisticated Pit Stops counterpart, spunky Kara was the short, buxom cheerleader that still managed to jump higher than all the rest just to put a smile on your face.

Funny, I'd always had a clear picture in mind as to Loren's forever person looked like - young, hip, childless, someone who would devote their lives to her. She got that in Stefan. With Kara, I wasn't sure who that person was. Someone that would give her unrelenting love and play fetch with her every day, for sure. Someone like Kyle, her foster mom, who I knew was struggling about giving her up. She loved the little chunk with all her heart. But Kyle already had a few too many dogs, not to mention the constant rotation of fosters, and her hubby wasn't keen on adding another to the pack.

These were my thoughts as we walked along motel row on a main street in Lafayette. My focus was broken by an immensely fat, freckled white woman who was sitting at the pool with her boyfriend, an incredibly buff black man with a skullcap and flashy designer sunglasses. She called over to Kara, so we went over for a quick pet. I told them Kara was a shelter dog from California, that she was a pit bull ambassador for my book tour.

"She looks like our dog that just died. We have two of her puppies," the woman told me. "After she'd had the puppies we'd put her outside to get back to normal, but she couldn't handle the cold. She died in February."

What? I thought. Are you kidding me? The woman looked sad and seemed to think I would be sympathetic. Instead the hair on the back of my neck stood up. I wanted to reach through the bars surrounding the pool and throttle her. Not only did she kill her dog, she was a breeder to boot.

"Well, I hope you never make that mistake again, now that you know what being out in the cold does to dogs," I said.

The woman blinked hard and didn't respond directly to my statement. "Well, your dog is really pretty," she said instead.

Rescue seems very futile when I meet people like that. For every dog we save, there's some idiot out there breeding 10 more, mistreating or in this case, killing, their primary dog.

As we headed back to the hotel, two young kids on bikes whizzed by. One said, "I like your dog!"

I screamed back, "Thanks! She's from the shelter!"

I waited until 8 p.m. to have dinner at Prejean's, a cavernous Cajun joint with live music, so that Kara would be comfortable waiting in the car as I enjoyed a rare meal at a restaurant. The majority of my meals were being eaten in the car or taken back to the hotel, so that Kara wouldn't be alone or suffer in the sweltering Southern heat.

To start, I had crunchy fried green tomatoes, served with a creamy, spicy shrimp and crawfish-laden sauce. That was so filling I only had room for a cup of the seafood gumbo, a rich, dark, intoxicating brew stocked with loads of crab, crawfish and shrimp, served with white rice. Delicious. Of course, I had to take some pralines to go. Prejean's has the best in all of the state: salty, sweet, nutty, buttery, completely addicting and just about the most amazing confection there is.

\*\*\*

Pit Stops 2

*"Squirrel?"*

In Jefferson, just outside of New Orleans, we stopped at LaFreniere Park, which I knew about from the first trip. It was close to our hotel and just magnificent: a huge, lushly landscaped oasis with water fountains and a looped little river surrounded by benches and bridges. Ducks and geese swam by or wandered the grounds confidently.

Kara was happily sniffing the grass when she spotted the first of several squirrels. She assumed the platypus pose and watched intently, ears at high alert, straining the leash ever so slightly. Had I let go, there's no doubt Kara would have ran right up the tree trying to catch it. Around the bend, a red and white goose watched us for a moment. I noticed the goose was wagging its little behind, just like Kara does, and laughed to myself.

It was just about dinner time, so I found an old-school seafood joint about five miles from our hotel and got a pound of boiled ruby red gulf shrimp to go. Yeah, I knew about the oil spill and all that, but honestly, seafood contamination was the least of my worries. Most of our food is polluted in one way or another. I'd still take my chances with locally sourced seafood over the known health risks of an overly processed Big Mac any day of the week.

The shrimp were large, tasty, plump, succulent, seasoned just right, served with buttery new potatoes and a long length of garlic bread, which allowed me to sop up all the juices. This was one of my favorite meals in the world. I went to bed happy, in a food coma, with Kara snuggled up at my side.

The next morning, we went to Café Freret in the city of New Orleans. A former home located in a residential neighborhood, Café Freret has a dog-friendly patio and complimentary, vet-formulated treats baked on the premises. Kara happily crunched on some peanut butter snacks while I tore into a decadent crab benedict, swimming in spicy hollandaise and complemented with crispy hash browns. Both of us were very satisfied.

Kara was a little anxious at first, but quickly settled down into café society, politely tolerating the several barky terriers that joined us on the patio. She watched calmly as a rather beat up calico cat stopped about ten feet in front of us and slowly laid down, as if it owned the place. I asked a waitress about the visitor.

"Oh yeah, that cat's like 20 years old. I didn't know cats could live that long," she said. "He lives down the street, in that yellow house. He's our most regular customer."

Well, the cat certainly wasn't afraid of Kara or any other canine presence that morning. He got up, walked into the middle of the patio and made himself right at home. The scene reminded me of the restaurant cats my sister and I met many, many years ago as we traveled throughout Greece.

On the way back, Kara and I drove through Bourbon Street. I knew better than to walk it again. That liquor-soaked stretch of tourist traps, bars and restaurants, with intoxicated people lining the streets, holds no appeal for me. People often assume because I am sober that I can't handle being around alcohol, that it might be tempting for me, but in fact the opposite is true. I just don't like being around drunks, loudness, impropriety or drama, plus the smell of alcohol makes me kind of ill. I find the bar scene, which Bourbon Street is to the extreme, simultaneously annoying and boring.

My idea of a good time was to hang out with rescue people, such as the amazing volunteers at Animal Rescue New Orleans. Loren and I had made some fantastic friends there.

Kara and I had a book signing scheduled at ARNO that afternoon from 3-6 p.m. and came at 2:30 to set up. The scorching Louisiana sun was bearing down hard and the accompany humidity had me sweating profusely. As for my hair, forget it. It was a fluffy mess on top of my head, no matter what attempts I made to restrain it.

Charlotte Bass Lilly, the executive director, had a canopy and table for us, and also made some tasty little sandwiches. I picked out the meat and gave it to Kara, who delicately ate the morsels.

"Are you a vegetarian now?" Charlotte asked me, almost incredulously.

"I try," I said. "I still eat seafood."

"Well, good for you. I can't do it, though. I like meat."

"I do, too," I said under my breath, looking wistfully at the pile of little muffuletta sandwiches. Then an image of a pig in a factory farm came to my mind and washed out whatever pleasure I would've taken in eating cold cuts. It was like getting sober. At first, my cravings for alcohol were pretty intense, but would go away in a matter of minutes. One meal at a time.

Traci Donellan Howerton brought cold lemonade and soda. Victoria Clark drove down with Traci. It was great to see them again. We all exchanged bear hugs and they oohed and aahed over Kara, who soaked up the attention like a big furry sponge.

Traci and her husband had adopted a baby boy and named him Cael. Now almost one, Cael smiled and cooed whenever he saw Kara and the other dogs who came by throughout the day.

"He already loves animals. I tell my husband that as soon as he can walk, I'm handing Cael a pooper scooper and putting him to work here," Traci said with a laugh.

Victoria showed me the new puppies ARNO recently rescued, which were being adopted over the weekend, chubby little terrier mixes, some more wiry than the others. She's an amazing girl, just 17, a junior in high school who's been volunteering at ARNO since she was 12. Victoria is mature beyond her years, especially when it comes to the animals she loves so dearly. Naturally, she wants to be a veterinarian.

Like Charlotte, Victoria spent the majority of the day inside, dealing with potential adopters. I was happy to see the hubbub, for the animals who were finding homes. ARNO really does great work out of that little industrial warehouse, saving about a thousand lives a year.

A volunteer named Tanya came to the signing. We hadn't met before, but quickly bonded as she told me her story. Tanya had been with ARNO since Hurricane Katrina. By day, Tanya worked for a local

## Back on the Bayou

food bank. As such, she frequently found herself in some of the rougher neighborhoods around New Orleans.

Not too long before, Tanya was driving when she spotted something. Not believing her eyes, she drove closer. It was a dog, a pit bull, hog tied to a pole in between two abandoned houses. The dog had three leather collars on its neck and its paws were roped through the collars. It couldn't sit. It was hanging three inches off the ground.

Tanya worked quickly to set the dog free. An elderly woman came by and watched. "Oh, I'm so glad you're here. That dog has been here for three days," the woman told Tanya.

"What? Why didn't you call anyone?" Tanya asked her. "How could you sleep at night, knowing this dog was out here, tied up like this?"

"Well, it was hard," the woman replied. "That dog would cry every night!"

Tanya shook her head, her expression vacillating between sad and furious. "I couldn't help it. I lost it and called her every name under the sun. If she hadn't been so old, I probably would've decked her," Tanya said.

Once freed, the dog drank every drop of the gallon of water Tanya had in the car. Since ARNO was full, Tanya was forced to take the dog, a large female, to the shelter. The dog would be euthanized the following Monday, unless a home or rescuer could be found.

Tanya thought she was at peace with the situation, that she had done all she could, yet it continued to torment her. She spoke of the dog to a friend, who had a friend that was a supporter of Villalobos Rescue Center, the rescue featured in Animal Planet's "Pit Bulls and Parolees." The woman had recently made a large donation to Villalobos and would see if the dog could be placed there.

Monday passed and Tanya was heartbroken, thinking the dog was dead. On Tuesday morning, she got word that Villalobos Rescue Center would take the dog, if she was still available. Tanya placed a call to the shelter and was happily surprised by the response.

"You know it was the weirdest thing. They were bringing your dog down the hall to be euthanized, when I had this feeling. I asked that the dog be given one more day," the shelter manager told Tanya. "I just had a feeling you would come through."

The dog, now named Gris Gris, was saved by Villalobos. Both Gris Gris and Tanya were featured in an episode of "Pit Bulls and Parolees." Gris Gris was still looking for a home as of the original air date.

"Wow," I told Tanya. "Sometimes I think I've heard it all, then I hear something like this. Thank God you saved that poor dog. You're a brave woman."

As we chatted, an ARNO alumni named Little Red and her owner, Bonnie, came by. Little Red is a little red and white pit bull mix that I met during our original trip to ARNO. She was a sweetheart, a Loren lookalike that waited a long time to find her person.

*"We're pretty lucky, huh, Little Red?"*

Bonnie, the young lady who adopted Little Red last September, clearly adored her. "She's just the best dog," Bonnie said, hugging Little Red close.

Kara and Little Red hit it right off, sniffing and kissing one another. Together they licked Cael's toes, as he giggled wildly from his stroller. Traci and I looked at them, then one another, sharing a silent moment of joy. These two former mama dogs were not only living a much better life, they were beautiful ambassadors for the breed.

# Lucky Dogs

To be a rescuer in L.A. is accepted, even admired by some. It's just another unique subculture in a colorful landscape of personalities. There are a lot of us and that strength in numbers is comforting. Smack dab in the middle of the South, a young woman named Ashley Owen Hill was working miracles on a daily basis. Largely alone.

Green was the primary color from the endless panorama of Southern foliage. A clear blue sky was the secondary hue as we drove from Louisiana to Meridian, Mississippi, where Ashley ran Lucky Dog Rescue. Kara and I had a signing there in the afternoon and were running on time, but my stomach was starting to growl. It was late morning and I desperately wanted a breakfast burrito, which was just about impossible to find in any parts past Texas.

We pulled up to a diner with a drive-thru and I was handed a thick menu to peruse. No breakfast burrito.

The waitress pulled out her pad and politely smiled at me, then gave Kara a big grin.

"Cute dog," she said.

"Thanks," I replied, scratching Kara's head. "Hey, do you have a breakfast burrito?"

"A what?" Her eyebrows raised.

"A breakfast burrito?"

"No we don't, sorry," she said in her slow southern drawl.

"Well, do you have a tortilla?" Maybe I could tell her how to make one.

She shook her head again.

I sighed. The things you take for granted living in Southern California, where breakfast burritos and other Mexican fare was available on just about every street corner. I missed it. The south was gorgeous and it had amazing seafood, but the humidity was a drag and the lack of breakfast burritos a crime.

Settling for an egg and cheese sandwich, I pulled over to a residential street and parked underneath a tree. Kara was languishing on her side, snoozing with the air conditioning vent pointed straight at her, ignoring my frantic feeding session. Outside it was practically dripping humidity, so I tried to keep us enclosed in this little sanctum as much as possible. My hair was already out of control and I knew Ashley was fond of taking pictures and posting them to Facebook. Yikes. It was bad enough that she was a pretty young blonde - now I was going to look a crazy-haired middle aged woman next to her.

Our little stop had taken us longer than expected, as did just about everything in the south. It seemed like people drove slower here, they definitely talked slower, and there was not the general sense of urgency I was used to dealing with back home. When we didn't have plans, it was fine, but that was rare. I had packed our schedule pretty tight.

"Alright, Pookie Lala," I said, wiping my mouth, tossing the container in my canvas trash bag and patting Kara's booty. "Let's get a move on."

If dogs could smile, I swear Kara grinned at me. She looked very content, even when I called her increasing silly pet names. I couldn't help it. Adore-a-bull Kara brought out the cooing maternal instinct in me.

The road to Lucky Dog was long, once we got off the highway exit, at least ten miles past town, where chain restaurants and motels abounded. It was a pretty drive, the surrounding areas lush with lawns that seemed to go on forever.

We made the turn to Lucky Dog and pulled up to a newer looking industrial building. In the front awaited Amy Ayers Mahoney, her husband Shannon, and their beautiful black and white bully girl, Daisy Dooley.

In addition to running Lucky Dog, Ashley also relentlessly networks dogs through Pet Pardons, a Facebook application she created with San Diego rescuer Chris Hoar. Pet Pardons, which has over 100,000 users, showcases death row dogs from across the country, letting its users automatically post pleas to their Facebook pages. That's where Amy and Shannon found Daisy.

They had recently lost their beloved dog Allie and wanted to adopt another in her honor. They planned to name her Daisy. Shortly thereafter, a black and white pit bull named Daisy appeared on Pet Pardons and the Mahoneys fell in love. It was Daisy's last day at the shelter. She was on the euth list.

Since Daisy was only available to be pulled by a rescue, a common practice for pits at city and county shelters, the Mahoneys contacted Ashley, who put a hold on her. The next day, Ashley pulled Daisy, who was very sick from heartworm, and the Mahoneys came from three hours away to pick her up.

*"Let's play helicopter! Whee!"*

The Mahoneys, who hadn't known what was going on with pit bulls in America's shelters, are now advocates for the breed, networking dogs on Facebook and sharing their experience with friends, family and anyone who will listen. They drove many hours to meet us and I was touched.

Daisy, a plucky little cutie, was still recovering from her illness, which may be why she wasn't that fond of Kara's wagging butt and intense sniffing upon their meet and greet.

"Sorry, she usually doesn't act like this," Amy said while Shannon pulled a growling Daisy back.

"Don't worry about it. She's probably just not in the mood. Kara can be a bit much sometimes," I said.

Ashley stepped out of the office, tall and tanned in a long black summer dress. She gave me a big hug before embracing Kara, who gave Ashley a series of sloppy kisses.

"Oh my God, I just love you!" Ashley said, kissing Kara back on top of her head. "Aren't you the cutest thing?"

"She is, huh?" I said, proudly. "It is so nice to finally meet you."

Ashley touched my arm. "Same here," she said. "Let me show you around, after we get Miss Kara comfortable."

We were led inside a clean, bare office with concrete floors where the desk had been cleared for me to set up books for the signing.

I handed Kara off to Kathy Penn, a volunteer, who immediately got down on the ground with Kara, hugging her close. Kathy, a 20-year old bartender studying to be a vet tech, was in love with Sissy, a black and white pit bull at Lucky Dog, and hoped to take her home, if her mother approved.

Until then, she was happy hanging out with Kara. "You are so pretty," Kathy fussed over Kara, who was now on her belly, happily receiving rubs.

Poor, deprived Kara, I laughed to myself, as I went to my car and unloaded. She was so unloved.

Inside, Ashley was checking her Blackberry, which seemed to chime about every minute. "I hope people come to this," Ashley said, her big blue eyes growing intense. "I asked everyone to support me. They better show up."

She looked like a sweet young thing, but I suspected there was a lot of steel in this magnolia.

"Don't worry, it's all good. Whoever shows up. I just hope I can raise some money for you," I said.

That was part of my reason for signing at rescues and shelters. Besides raising awareness, I had created a fundraising mechanism through the sale of a special Loren "limited edition" bookmark.

It featured a painting of Loren by Melinda Dalke, a marvelous artist out of Oregon and yet another Facebook friend. The painting had Loren's face against a backdrop of Pittsburgh attractions and said "Pit Stops." I charged $5 for the bookmark, of which I gave 100 percent of the proceeds to our host rescue or advocacy organization.

Once I was set up, there was still a little time before the signing, so Ashley gave me a brief tour. Lucky Dog was a very nice facility, with indoor/outdoor kennels, air-conditioned to protect its boarders and residents from the sweltering Southern heat.

The kennels were set on several picturesque acres, surrounded by nature trails. One side of the main building was designated for boarders, the other for rescues.

*The handsome, irrepressible Lucky*

As we toured the rescue side, a dozen beautiful pit bulls in all sizes and colors greeted me. Lucky, who had one blue eye and one brown eye, looked up adoringly at Ashley as she kneeled down and scratched him through the chain link. He had a gimpy front paw and barely any ears to speak of from a homemade crop job gone wrong. A shelter worker in Louisville, Mississippi, where Lucky was dumped, had called Ashley in the desperate hope that she could help. She did, of course. Lucky was Lucky Dog's first official rescue and the inspiration for its name.

"He was just such a sweetheart. He really tugs at your heart strings," Ashley said, getting a kiss from Lucky now. "I had to take him in."

"You're amazing," I told Ashley, impressed. "This is an incredible set up. I know it's a lot of work. I really look forward to helping you tomorrow."

"You really don't have to," Ashley said, standing up and heading back towards the office.

"Are you kidding? It'll be the highlight of our trip. I love picking up poop. It's what I live for."

Ashley chuckled. "Then you'll like it here."

People were starting to show up. Ashley writes a column for The Meridian Star and promoted the signing. The first to arrive was a stout, older man wearing a trucker cap and a meek, mousy woman with no makeup, glasses and plain light blue pants with a cream-colored shirt.

"Sit," he instructed the woman as one would a dog. She promptly sat. Ashley and I looked at another in bemused horror.

The man pulled out a book that looked like it had been written in the 1950's called "The American Pit Bull Terrier." He proceeded to go on and on about pit bulls and dogs in general in a dry professorial way, while his wife sat on her hands and looked down at the ground.

Ashley finally broke the spell. "Umm, that's great, are you here to get a book? Learn more about boarding? What can we do for you?"

The man handed Ashley the book. "Well, I knew you like dogs, so I wanted you to have this and I'd like to get a book, too."

Ah, the first sale of the day. It was a weird sensation, having people interested in my book, about me & Loren's adventures, to find that anyone even cared at all. It wasn't like I was a celebrity or anything. Sick thing was, if I was some reality star, I could write a book about nothing and it would sell 250,000 copies in weeks. People like me, on the other hand, had to fight for every sale. Only 5 percent of self-published authors ever broke even, let alone had a successful book on their hands.

Sometimes I dreamt of being on Oprah, of getting that big break, not so much for the money or fame, but so I could have the freedom to spend all my time helping dogs, not schlepping it out at the paper, which I knew had a limited future and paid less than desirable wages, especially for someone that lived in expensive Southern California. In the meantime, I was determined to be one of the 5 percent, one book at a time.

I signed while Kara wiggled her butt and hugged on knees, making friends immediately and prompting smiles all around. All told, about 12 copies of "Pit Stops" were sold that day, to Ashley's friends and family, to pit bull lovers she knew on Facebook, to Lucky Dog supporters and a Meridian official who knew of Ashley's immense efforts to helping dogs in the area, such as volunteering with the local spay/neuter clinic and starting a dog house drive for low-income families.

"Wow, Ashley's an amazing young woman," I said to the man. "I hope you support her on a legislative or political level any way you can. These animals really need your help, too."

"I'll do my best," he said.

Throughout the signing, Ashley was eagerly anticipating a new arrival, a ten year old female pit bull named June Bug, who was rechristened Melody by the shelter volunteer who originally alerted Ashley about the dog. Melody made it late in the afternoon, a tan beauty with more than a few signs of wear. She was running about the dog run when we entered and ran over to Ashley, who immediately bent down to hug her.

"Hi sweetheart, hi Melody," Ashley cooed to the very grateful dog, who tucked herself between Ashley's arms and lap, shyly soaking up the love.

I pet her too, my hand running over the skinny ribs covered by lackluster fur and more than a few scars. Poor thing.

"We named her after 'Unchained Melody,' because she spent her whole life on a chain," Ashley said, shaking her head in anger. "Melody's family lost their house during the tornado in Huntsville, yet Melody survived. The shelter took her and contacted the family, but they didn't want her back. Can you

*"Thanks for saving me, Ashley."*

imagine?"

Indeed, I could, and it horrified me, the image of a dog chained to the ground during one of the most powerful hurricanes on record. I pictured the skinny, golden, graying pit bull flailing about in the wind, terrified, left to deal with her residual fear, alone and hungry, for days, only to be rejected and slated for death because her family once again failed her.

Unfortunately, every time I think I've heard it all, something still manages to shock me.

\*\*\*

The rolling hills were calling Kara's name. Our hotel, located in the middle of town, was not fetch-friendly, but the front lawn of Lucky Dog Resort and Rescue certainly was. We rolled out of bed, ate a quick breakfast and hustled out for our volunteering session.

The weather was staggeringly muggy, the kind of humidity that enveloped you in a shiny film of sweat from the moment you dared step outside. Kara was unfazed. As soon as we got out of the car and she saw the Frisbee, it was game on. My Frisbee skills are not the best, so half the time it would land with a thud a few feet in front of us or roll down the hill like a wheel. But there were a few moments when that disc would soar just right and Kara would catch it mid-flight, delighting us both. That stocky body became something graceful and supremely

*"Look what I got!"*

athletic as Kara sailed through the air. It was a beautiful sight.

Ashley pulled up in her grey Toyota Camry, wearing shorts and a tank top, still managing to look fantastic in this Southern sweatbox. Maybe you had to be born there and acclimate your whole life in order to keep up a decent appearance?

She smiled when she saw us. "Are you sure you want to do this?" Ashley asked. "It's awful hot."

"Of course," I said. "I do this all the time at home. It gets pretty hot at Brittany Foundation, like 105. I'll be fine." I left out that it was a proverbial dry heat while the humidity here threatened to suffocate me.

"Alright. Let's go."

First, we situated Kara in the air-conditioned office. Kyle's large crate came in handy, it was like a doggy condo. I laid the fluffy dog bed down, then added a bowl of water in the corner, and Kara went right in. Since I've never crate-trained my dogs, I always felt guilty putting any dog in a crate. Kyle assured me Kara liked it and sure enough, she laid down, crossed her paws, and looked perfectly content.

"We'll be back, girl. You enjoy this nice cold room," I said, putting my face next to the bars for a kiss. Kara stood up, obliged, then looped around, settling with a sigh. I envied her. A nap already sounded good to me, too. I was not sleeping very well on this trip so far.

A volunteer had already let out many of the dogs for play time, but there was still plenty of cleaning to do. Ashley grabbed a canister of blue pet-friendly cleaner, a hose and a long-handled squeegee. The dogs were led to the outdoor portion of the kennel. Ashley would close the guillotine door and pick up the poop with a scooper. She showed me how to spray down the concrete floors, scrubbing to remove some of the stubborn stains, followed by a hosing process. Lucky Dog had a convenient drain/trough that captured the runoff.

"Having fun yet?" Ashley asked me with a wink.

"Good times," I replied with a smile. "I can't believe you do this every day. You're one tough cookie."

Ashley had been independently rescuing and fostering shelter dogs or taking in strays for close to a decade, since she was 16. She opened Lucky Dog in October of 2010. A former pharmaceutical sales representative, Ashley took a two-thirds pay reduction to do so, wishing to fulfill her personal goals instead of pursuing financial security. She is

Lucky Dog's sole employee, with intermittent help from a small corps of volunteers.

"It's hard work but I love it. This has been my dream since I was a little kid. I was in a near-fatal car accident when I was 18 and decided then that I didn't want to wait to live my life," she said. "I'd been looking for a kennel for a long time before I found this place. The boarding dogs help pay for the rescue."

Once we were done with the kennels, Ashley and I walked Capone, a hound pit mix, and Missy, a big golden mixed breed, youngsters who love to play and get their leashes in a tangle. They dragged us down the trail, sniffing with joy all the way. It was stiflingly hot, but the dogs were in heaven.

Capone was a shelter rescue and Missy was left behind by people who found her on the side of the road and promised to find her a home, asking Ashley to board the dog for a few days. When no homes came through, they offered to take Missy to a shelter.

"Of course, I couldn't let that happen," Ashley said, rolling her eyes.

Instead, Missy will remain at Lucky Dog until she finds her forever home. Ashley takes one dog from the rescue home with her each evening to acclimate them to a regular household routine and make them more adoptable. All Lucky Dog adopters have to fill out an application, pay a fee of $100 and submit to a home check.

It was clear Ashley loved interacting with the dogs. Susie, a black and white pit bull, was saved from a life of breeding and certain death at the shelter. The three of us were taking a play break in one of Lucky Dog's large enclosed runs.

Tired of ball, Susie came up to Ashley and flopped herself on the grass to do a roly poly. Ashley beamed, flashing brilliant white teeth. "She just loves to do that. It's her favorite thing. Isn't it, mama?" she said, reaching down to rub her belly with its protruding nipples.

"Lucky, Susie, all these dogs, had nowhere else to go. That breaks my heart," Ashley continued, now with tears in her eyes. "A lot of them had never known love before. It's a drop in the bucket, I know, but at least they have a chance here. They have a life."

I gave her a hug and she embraced me back. "It's huge what you're doing, Ashley. Huge." We parted. Enough with the mush. There were dogs to be walked.

Across the way, six outdoor kennels with dog houses were situated under a large, shaded awning. Each was occupied by a singular pit bull, including a girl named Bonnie, a super-size Kara lookalike. These dogs were scheduled to be confiscated and killed from a fellow rescuer after a neighbor complained and the county threatened to enforce its recently enacted breed specific legislation. Once again, Ashley answered the call and stepped up to the plate.

"Eventually, I want to expand and add more kennels and fenced yards," she told me, pointing across the picturesque land. "Rescue more dogs."

A few hours later, after we worked up an appetite to match our sweat, Ashley and I had lunch at a local deli, leaving Kara to continue lounging in climate-controlled comfort. Ashley ordered a salad and I had a baked potato with steamed vegetables and chile-spiked cheese sauce. Like most of the rescuers I meet, Ashley is a vegetarian.

"This is such a treat for me," I told Ashley. "I've been eating inside my car or in hotel rooms for two weeks now."

"It's nice for me, too, to have someone I can relate to. My friends think I'm kind of crazy," she said. "Most of them are having babies now. At one of the showers, a friend of mine told me she was going to breed her dog. The one she bought from a breeder!"

I shuddered. This was dangerous territory for advocates and rescuers. My friend Yvonne ended a decade-long friendship after her friend bought a puppy from a pet store.

"I couldn't believe it. She knows who I am and what I do. I tried to talk her out of it, but she just kept looking at me kind of blankly," Ashley said, biting her lip for a second. "Everyone just carried on at the shower like nothing was wrong, but I felt like I was dying inside. It's like I have nothing in common with these people."

"You know, as you get older, you'll find that friends grow apart and that there's really only a few people that truly get you because you finally get yourself," I said, the wise elder. After all, I could be Ashley's mother, if I'd had her at 16. When did I get so old? "Face it, I just don't think you're that white picket fence, baby shower kind of girl. You're a rescuer…a hardcore one…and it's OK."

Ashley beamed. "See, you get it…it's so nice to talk to someone who gets it!"

"I know, right?" I said, grinning back. "It can be kind of lonely sometimes."

I had been feeling pretty low before our visit to Meridian. Sitting with Ashley at that chain deli, both of us grubby and grimy and not caring whatsoever about our appearance, sharing our experiences, lifted the dark cloud that had been in my head since Kara and I left. Exposing the things that weighed on my soul with someone that truly understood was exactly what I needed.

Like me, Ashley worried about how to most effectively spend her time. Was it advocating more spay/neuter? Working with government officials on legislation that will help these dogs at the shelter level? Providing resources to low-income owners to keep dogs in the home? Cracking down on backyard breeders, which in her neck of the woods, were a dime a dozen? How do you reach out to a seemingly uncaring or unknowing public?

The latter is one of the reasons Ashley helped to start Pet Pardons. "You hear about these huge numbers, that millions of dogs are killed at shelters every year, but people can ignore that. When you see their faces and know this dog will die, it just connects so much more. People start to care. The more people you get involved, the closer you get to solving the problem," she told me.

Surprisingly, Pet Pardons, and Ashley in particular, have come under attack from some within the rescue community. First, it was because a few unscrupulous people used Pet Pardons to falsely raise funds for dogs they didn't actually rescue. Once Ashley was alerted to the situation, she immediately had preventative controls put in place to prohibit such practices. Still, Ashley consistently received negative emails and posts, ranging from rude to threatening.

I'd seen these attacks before and always rose to Ashley's defense, even though we hadn't met yet. I just intuitively knew she was the real deal and now, after meeting her, I will defend Ashley's name to the end. This girl not only walks her talk, she's devoted her whole life to saving dogs and consistently goes above and beyond the call of duty. Most impressively, Ashley still managed to be sane and articulate. It will come as no surprise to me when Ashley becomes a recognized leader in the national animal welfare movement. She was already well on her way.

Though she looked comfy lounging in her crate in the air-conditioned office, Kara was very happy to see us return, wiggling her booty at maximum speed. Ashley let her out and gave Kara some love while I tended to loading up the car.

We quickly hugged. Ashley turned around and walked straight back into the building, a rather abrupt goodbye, but I knew she had work to do. I was just sad to leave this place and this brave young woman who helped set me right again after I was almost ready to give up the fight.

"Alright, Kare Bear. On to Florida," I said. She looked back at me, gold eyes shining, ready for the next adventure. My fearless little road buddy.

The next day I awoke to a wonderful surprise. Ashley, who's a very moving writer, had honored us in her Lucky Dog Rescue blog. I read a passage aloud to Kara:

*"Michelle's visit was really special to me. While I knew we'd get along, I didn't realize just how much I'd connect with her... and the massive appreciation I'd have for that connection. Sometimes, you don't realize how alone you are... until you're not alone anymore. Even though she wasn't here for long... our time together was enough to recharge my battery... to remind me that other people in this world "get it," and that they're out there fighting just like I am. I needed that reminder."*

Hugging Kara, I cried, humbled by this once virtual stranger who now felt more like a little sister.

## Hello Dolly

I don't know if I've ever made a more embarrassing first impression than I did with Erica Daniel of Dolly's Foundation.

I was friends with Erica on Facebook, but had we never met in person before. She was a young blonde, just 26 (like Ashley) and a real crusader for pit bulls.

Our plan was to meet at Outback Steakhouse, right across the street from our rather shady motel in Sanford, Florida. Kara and I had arrived earlier that day and I was slightly horrified by the tacky Vegas décor. Kara, however, was unfazed. She jumped right on that rainbow-striped satin bedspread and immediately made herself comfortable. It was naptime for her, laundry time for me.

Clouds were gathering about 10 minutes before our dinner date with Erica, little sprinkles filling the air before turning into rather large splotches.

"Hurry up, Kara!" I said impatiently.

We were on a large grassy stretch outside the hotel, taking a potty break. Like Loren, Kara liked to take her time at the most inopportune moments. Mission accomplished, we both sprinted to the car. Thunder and lightning had taken over the sky and now, the rain was really falling, the start of an epic Southern summer storm.

This didn't bode well. Kyle had warned me that Kara was afraid of loud noises and I had to leave her in the car. Images of my new interior ripped up by a frantic Kara was weighing on me as I planned my exit from the car to the restaurant.

What should be like a short easy trip to the patio was now daunting, considering it was Friday night in the suburbs, a holiday weekend, too. The lot was packed so I parked towards the back, about 100 yards from the restaurant, and waited for the storm to subside. Problem was, it was only getting worse.

"Wow, Kara. This is insane!"

She looked at me, ears at full mast, eyes blinking nervously every time the thunder cracked.

## Hello Dolly

"I'm so sorry I have to leave you, but at least you don't have to go out in this."

Searching her bag, I found a Nylabone to keep Kara occupied. She settled on the fuzzy pink blanket and began chewing.

"Be a good girl," I said, kissing her velvet head. She licked me and went back to her bone. "Wish me luck."

Holding my breath, I opened the door and ducked out into the black rainy night towards the brightly lit restaurant. I felt like a cartoon character being held under a moving waterfall as I sprinted through immense puddles that splashed up to my knees. My feet were now completely soaked. By the time I made it to the patio, my Levis and long-sleeved black Social Distortion shirt were plastered to my skin. I could've wrung my clothes and at least a gallon of water would've come out.

"Michelle?" I heard a voice call out from the darkness.

"Yes. Erica?"

"Yes," she said and stepped out into the light. Erica, who was perfectly dry, wore a white Dolly's Foundation t-shirt. Her cute blonde locks hung straight to her shoulders and she boasted a big smile. How did these Southern girls keep their hair so perfect under conditions like these? Seriously.

"Oh, you poor thing," she said, hugging me, the drowned rat.

"Yeah, I'm a little embarrassed," I said, trying not to soak her. "Not exactly the way I like to first meet someone. I wasn't expecting a hurricane."

Erica giggled, albeit politely. "Welcome to Florida. I put our name in for a table."

"OK, I'm going to run to the restroom and try to dry off. See you in a few minutes."

I really have a love hate/thing with the south. It's such gorgeous country, so green and lush, and the people were so friendly. Yet weird things always seemed to happen to me, such as the camping trip that had preceded my meeting with Erica.

Since Kara and I had successfully made it through two nights in Louisiana, I thought Florida would be a snap. I wouldn't let the memory of an itsy bitsy snake wriggling around my foot hold me back from exploring one of the prettiest areas in the country.

Caverns State Park was just off the road from the charming town of

Marianna, which boasts historic buildings and mom and pop cafes in additional to the usual McDonalds and Waffle House so familiar to travelers. Humidity was so strong in places that store windows were layered with a thick haze of condensation.

After grilling the park ranger, I was happy to learn that a) alligators were known to congregate in a river at least a mile from our campgrounds and b) there was a camp host on site. Kara and I drove to the Blue Hole campground and selected a spot conveniently close to the host and a huge, clean, quiet bathroom. The grounds were beautiful, with red earth beneath our feet and thousands of tall, skinny trees and curling, flourishing vines.

I set up the tent and air mattress lightning fast and let Kara off leash to play some catch. She was the only dog in the park, which was about one quarter occupied. Kara minded so well, I felt very comfortable setting her free to explore our small space. All I had to do was call her name if she got more than 10 feet away and she'd trot right back over.

We were the only tent campers, everyone else had RVs. It was sweltering, in the 90's, but we did our best to relax for a few before heading back into town to poach a WIFI channel and get some provisions.

It was pretty comfortable inside our tent. The sun was going down, a breeze circulating through the mesh windows. I had a good book, a lantern to read by and little Kara snuggled by my feet. There were no ducks quacking, just the occasional cricket and bird sounds. For camping, it was pretty peaceful.

At about 10 p.m., just as I was drifting off to sleep, the phone rang. It was Wayde in California, three hours behind us. Of course, I was happy to hear his voice, but I was a bit mad, too, since sleep can be illusory for me once I'm awakened. We recapped our day, quickly, so I could get back to bed.

Out of nowhere came a long, piercing bird call. Was there a wild macaw on the loose? Ha. That wasn't going to be enough to scare us.

An hour later, we both heard it, the unmistakable sound of something moving about the dead leaves, precariously close to our tent. Crunch, crunch, crunch. It got louder and louder.

I stopped breathing to listen.

## Hello Dolly

Kara's ears not only stood straight up, she jumped from my feet and crawled up to my neck, placing her head next to mine. It stopped for a minute, as did my heart when the sound continued just a few moments later.

I pictured a huge, flat-footed alligator, its long tail dragging in the leaves, cruising around the campground in search of a meal. I could see it coming to our little tent, blowing its hot breath precariously close to us. Separated only by a millimeter of nylon, Kara and I didn't stand a chance.

*"What was that?"*

My heart started beating faster until it became a steady hammer in my chest. Kara moved up from my neck and sat on my head. I've been taught to say the serenity prayer in times of trouble, so I did:

God, grant me the serenity to accept the things I cannot change...*We're in the middle of the Florida woods, possibly with an alligator hot at our heels.*

The courage to change the things I can...*We're getting the hell out of here and into a hotel. Now.*

And the wisdom to know the difference…*It may not be wise, this may not be an alligator, I may be a total freak, but it's midnight and there's no way I or this dog will ever be able to sleep with the possibility of being eaten by a reptile.*

Frantically searching about for my glasses, cell phone, sandals and the leash, I clumsily unzipped the tent. Kara hopped out, followed by me and we beat a quick retreat to the comfort of the RAV4. I looked around the campground and heard the scurrying again. Stifling the urge to scream, I quickly observed that all the other campers were safely ensconced in their RVs, completely oblivious to our drama unfolding outside. Lucky bastards.

I turned on the car, consulted the GPS for nearby hotels and found a Days Inn, which was pet-friendly, about seven miles away. Never had I been so happy to see a bed in my life. Neither had Kara, I think. We both sank into the mass of fluffy white pillows and blankets, exhaling at the same time. I heard Kara snoring soon thereafter, though I was still up for much of the night, feeling very far from home, literally and figuratively.

We had to go back in the morning to retrieve our camping equipment. I told the park ranger on duty what happened and as he processed my refund, he kindly told me that most likely the creature I was fearing was an armadillo.

"They scurry around at night and sound a lot bigger than they are," he said, sympathetically.

"Yeah, well, when it's you and dog in a tent and there's a possibility, however remote, that a gator could be in your vicinity, it's hard to stay rational," I said. "I don't necessarily want to meet an armadillo in the middle of the night, either."

"I don't blame you for being freaked out."

"Thank you for being so nice."

We stayed in the hotel most of that day, so I could catch up on laundry and Signal stories, which I was still writing at the rate of two per week. There was a Po' Folks restaurant (imagine a hyper-Southern version of Denny's) across the way which had a pick and choose vegetable plate. Problem was, at least half the options had ham or bacon. I went with a mass o' starch: mashed potatoes, macaroni and cheese, and corn, topped off with a biscuit. Not my healthiest culinary moment, but it hit the spot. Earlier that morning I finally went to a

## Hello Dolly

Waffle House for the first time, ordering an omelet and some hash browns to go. The food was passable, but nothing like the phenomenon I'd read about from passionate food bloggers and patrons on Yelp.

Hotel fetch had to do, since I couldn't find an outdoor spot. A rolled up sock filled in as a ball. Though Kara had been sent off with at least three toys, and I'd bought about a half dozen along the way, there were none left. Her first Kong was resting indefinitely under a shed in a Texas La Quinta parking lot after I threw it too far. I had tried to retrieve it, but once I saw the debris and mystery critters living under that shed, I decided to invest in another one instead. Kara ate the flexible Frisbee I bought in Louisiana, as well as another Frisbee in Santa Fe. Two tennis balls had disappeared. So I got creative, molding the sock ball and throwing it about the hotel. Kara didn't mind. It was just the thrill of the chase for her.

Sometimes, people ask me why I travel with a dog and not another human being. This is why. Dogs are flexible, accommodating and never whine. Traveling across country is not always fun or glamorous, believe me, at least not on my budget. There's the packing and unpacking every day or other day. Weird weather and wild animals. Eating on the run. Setting up for signings. It can be trying and the thought of navigating these challenges with a person, with their own needs and notions of how to do things, is too much, at least for me. Dogs are much easier.

It helped that Kara was the absolute sweetest dog around. Nothing got her down. She just wiggled her butt and got on with it. Slept a lot. Enjoyed the small things, like seeing wayward ducks or scurrying squirrels, sniffing a new patch of grass or playing a game of fetch in a hotel room with a rolled up sock or snuggling with her auntie.

She didn't laugh at my clumsiness, like when I spilled half a huge cup of iced tea down the

*"Sock fetch? Works for me!"*

front of my shorts while trying to concoct an Arnold Palmer in the car. (Wayde calls Arnold Palmers my crack and it's true. Until I get that first hit off the straw, like an addict hitting the pipe, my day hasn't really begun).

Nor did she bat an eye when I accidentally closed the car door on my take-out breakfast one morning in Marianna, aptly called the junk plate. The fantastic concoction of potatoes, cheese, onions, green peppers and fried eggs escaped its Styrofoam container and slid into the plastic bag. Kara didn't gross out as I hurriedly slurped up the hash browns and possibly tainted eggs from the bag.

Nor did she complain about having to get the car serviced at a little country dealership, whiling away the time by conversing with a stranger about war and politics.

Nope, Kara was happy just to be, wherever and with whomever. This is why I love dogs. They can teach us humans a lot.

\*\*\*

At dinner, Erica listened intently as I shared our camping adventures and general travails on the road. The girl was very gracious, even after I accidentally called her Jen. I was getting all my Facebook friends confused, mistaking Erica for Jen Carle, whom I was due to meet in Baltimore.

"I'm so sorry. I'm a little frazzled."

"Don't worry about it," Erica assured me.

I was sticking to the vinyl booth like a decal on a hot car window. I tried to put the fact that I was soaking wet and looked like a complete idiot out of my mind while Erica gave me the background on how Dolly's Foundation came about.

Erica worked by day as a kennel attendant at a central Florida shelter. She'd heard every excuse in the book by wayward, reckless, uncaring owners while the canine body count stacked up. Sick of it, Erica began countering with solution.

Take the pit bull owner whose dogs were confiscated after he went to jail. When the man, whom Erica said looked like Lil' John, came back to retrieve three of the four dogs from the shelter, Erica asked him why he didn't want them all back.

## Hello Dolly

"He said he had seven more at home. I asked him if he bred puppies and he said yes. So I told him that most of the pit bulls here were a result of backyard breeding and that many of them would die in a shelter just like this one. He seemed shocked, asking me, 'For real?' Then I told him about spaying and neutering, that dogs who don't get fixed often get cancer, and he just kept saying, 'For real?'"

While Erica, who has a degree in zoology, never heard back from the rapper look-alike, and doesn't know if her education efforts always make an impact, she never stops trying.

Sometimes she scores a direct hit.

When a young couple walked into the shelter six months prior, Erica asked them what kind of dog they were looking for. "Anything but a pit bull," the woman replied.

Erica spent time with the couple, educating them about the breed and introducing them to many of the shelter's available dogs. Twenty minutes later, the couple walked out with a pit bull. They emailed Erica shortly thereafter with the happy news. "This is the best dog we've ever had!"

That kind of story brings a smile to Erica's face. So does Dolly, the pit bull she rescued more than a year ago from the shelter. Dolly had come in, mangy, scarred and bloody from a stint as a bait dog, the passive pawn used to train other dogs how to fight. Erica, who admits to having a strong affection for the hardest luck stories, immediately felt a kinship to Dolly and took her home to heal.

The Daniel home is on a two-acre spread in Geneva, where Dolly now lives with four other dogs and Erica's husband, Grant. Dolly has not only recovered from the trauma, she blossomed into a snow-white beauty that now represents her breed as a canine good citizen at appearances at nursing homes and children's hospitals throughout Sanford.

Inspired by Dolly, Erica started Dolly's Foundation in January and quickly garnered support from pit bull lovers all over the world through Facebook. DF, as she calls it, has thousands of friends, many of whom send donations and gifts such as homemade dog collars that the organization sells to raise funds.

In April 2011, Best Friends Animal Society asked Erica and Dolly to appear in Tallahassee on behalf of Bill SB722, which would overturn the current "dangerous dog" law and allow shelters to evaluate and rehabilitate dogs used in fighting rings rather than automatically euthanizing them.

"Several of the representatives were on the fence and asked me for my opinion. I said, 'Look at my dog,'" Erica said. "I showed them the before and after pix of Dolly, told them that she was a CGC and therapy dog, that she does wonderful things for her breed."

SB722 unanimously passed.

A fifth grade girl in Sanford had heard about Dolly. Inspired, she wrote a speech about the dog to present in class. Erica planned to surprise the youngster with a visit from Dolly that upcoming Sunday. "Dolly's just the best advocate for her breed," Erica said proudly.

*Erica Daniel and Dolly at the SB722 hearing in Tallahassee, Florida*

Since its inception, DF has saved more than a dozen pit bulls from shelters in the area and placed them in foster or adoptive homes. The happy endings kept Erica going when the harsh reality of what happens to many pit bulls at the shelter, where the breed makes up anywhere from 70 to 80 percent of the canine residents, became too much.

## Hello Dolly

As a kennel attendant, Erica nursed the dogs' wounds, gave them attention and cheered when one got adopted into a good home. She hoped for the best when adopters didn't seem to have the dogs' best interest at heart. (Home checks were not required at the open-door shelter, which takes in 14,000 animals a year).

"It's really hard," Erica said with a sigh. "I'd say a dog has skin issues or an expensive health condition or isn't good with kids. I'd try to talk them out of it."

Due to lack of space at the shelter, pit bulls were usually the first dogs selected to be killed. Erica was often in the room during the euthanasia process.

"I'd give them special treats or a walk or just sit in the sunshine with them," Erica said. "I give every dog I can a bath before they are put down. They need to know what it's like to be clean, to die with dignity."

The thought of a dog like Kara, an innocent sweetheart of a soul, being put down for nothing more than lack of space at a shelter was almost more than I could bear. That Erica could help homeless, unwanted dogs meet their end with love and compassion earned my respect and broke my heart at the same time. She was a truly brave woman.

My eyes filled with tears, which Erica quickly noticed. "Stop it, you're going to make me cry," she said and sure enough, her eyes got misty.

After working a long day at the shelter, Erica spent many of her remaining waking hours transporting dogs to fosters, raising funds for heartworm treatments and networking on Facebook, in addition to taking care of her own pack, which currently includes a foster pit bull named Tecky, whom Erica rescued out of the shelter.

"I can't sleep at night, thinking of all the dogs," she said. "I'm obsessed with it, with trying to help."

When I asked what her ultimate goal was for Dolly's Foundation, the spunky blonde 26-year old didn't hesitate. "Global domination," Erica said with a laugh, though her eyes glowed with intense determination. "It's all about education. One person at a time."

\*\*\*

The next day was largely open, so I decided to make the most of it. "How about a spa day, Kara?" I asked the slumbering dog, rubbing her belly as we prepared to get out of bed. It was a longer process than usual as I had a hard time separating myself from Kara, who became like a second appendage during the course of the evening.

I looked up a groomer for Kara and a masseuse for me. Once I found both, we headed towards the newer part of town, full of shiny new shopping centers, to PetSmart. Kara was received with much fanfare by the young groomer, which made me happy. So far, we hadn't encountered any pit bull prejudice. There was no running away or crossing the street to get away from us, like I'd experienced with Loren. If anything, people were intrigued by Kara and many didn't even realize she was a bully breed until I told them.

My masseuse, a kind Jamaican woman, had an office located in an older section of the downtown, which was rife with brick and white pillars in between older industrial buildings. The shimmering waterfront, I imagined, was loaded with gators so I stayed far away.

It was heaven getting those kinks worked out of my neck, shoulders and back. The hour long massage left me mellow, relaxed and hungry. I headed to The Corner Cafe, a modern-looking little bistro where I enjoyed a stellar, refreshing cup of tomato basil soup, a crispy, cheesy roasted vegetable panini and a tiny "shot" of peanut butter and chocolate mousse, which the kind young cashier gave to me on the house.

Not surprisingly, back at PetSmart, Kara had completely wooed the groomers, earning a gold star on her checkout sheet. "She's a great dog," the groomer told me as Kara hugged her goodbye.

I bent down to smell her, taking in the fresh scent of lavender, and kissed the top of Kara's head. "Pookie Lala. Such a pretty girl and now you smell good, too!" Now I needed some grooming before the book signing and "Pints for Pits" event scheduled with Erica and Dolly's Foundation.

The drive to Geneva from Sanford was longer than I expected, leading us into some long stretches of green country roads. Finally, we arrived at the Daniel home. Erica, who was loading the bed of her Toyota Tundra, ran out to open the long wooden gate for us. The Daniel's log cabin-style home was set on plush acreage. It would fit right into Pine Mountain Club.

## Hello Dolly

Grant, Erica's husband, came out of the garage to greet me. With his dark brown hair, goatee and wiry build, Grant reminded me a lot of Wayde. That notion was enforced when I saw the large change bottle emblazoned with "8" in the garage.

"Nascar fan, huh?" I asked Grant as Erica took Kara for a quick potty break.

"Yeah," he said.

"My boyfriend is, too," I said. "We have a big red number 9 hood in our garage."

Grant nodded and smiled. His demeanor was pretty similar to Wayde's, the strong silent type. Interesting. He and Erica appeared to be the introvert and the extrovert, the classic Yin and Yang. Just like me and Wayde.

Erica came over with Kara and handed me the leash.

"I'm going inside to check on the dogs," she said. "Be right back."

I looked at Grant. "You sure you don't mind watching Kara while

*"Is it hot out here or is it just me?"*

we're out?"

"No, I don't mind at all," Grant said, kneeling down and allowing Kara to cover his face in kisses. He hugged her close. She was in good hands.

"Kara tends to poop around 7 p.m. and then she's fine," I said and laughed. "What can I say? You get to know someone pretty well after a few weeks of traveling…"

"No problem," Grant said.

Erica ushered us into their lovely home, which had high-beam ceilings, hardwood floors and a warm, cozy feel.

"Wow, this is really nice," I told them, truly impressed.

"Thanks," Erica said. "Let's put Kara in the crate and you can meet the dogs."

There was a large wire crate in the corner, in the living room, with a comfy blanket and a bowl of water. Kara climbed right in. I dropped the Nylabone through a slot and patted her furrowed forehead.

"You're gonna be fine, Kare Bear," I said, calmly, before getting up and following Erica. Crating was always hard for me, though I found it to be a very common practice amongst rescuers. The dogs didn't seem to mind it; most of them seemed to like it.

So I tried not to be too dramatic when saying goodbye or too guilty for leaving Kara in a strange place, yet again. It was weird, putting trust in people you didn't really know with a dog that wasn't yours, but in the universe I found myself in, everything always turned out just fine. So I went with it.

Erica opened some French doors to another room, where there were a couple of crates, one containing a very familiar face. The snow-white dog with cropped ears and a heart-shaped outline on her nose looked at me calmly, her paws crossed like a proper lady.

"Oh, Dolly," I said as Erica beamed.

"Isn't she just beautiful?" she asked proudly.

"She really is."

Next to Dolly was a black and white boy with floppy ears who tilted his head and got a little excited upon our entrance.

## Hello Dolly

"That's Tecky, he's our foster. I adore him. He's such a great dog," Erica said. "I don't know why he hasn't found a home yet. Tecky's awesome."

We walked to the master bedroom where a senior Dachshund named Clifford reigned supreme, outstretched on the large mattress.

Erica checked her watch. "We gotta go," she said, giving Grant a quick kiss and moving towards the front door. "See you later?"

*"Who's the nice lady with the crazy hair?"*

"Yes," Grant said, settling back on the couch, watching a Nascar race on the big-screen TV. From her crate, Kara looked at me, then Grant, before turning her attention back to the Nylabone. She was going to be just fine.

I followed Erica to the truck. We hopped in and Erica started moving stuff to the back cab. "Sorry," she said, working fast to clear out space for me.

Rescuers. They all had the same cars, it seemed, stuffed full of banners and materials and buttons and dog food, clothes and toys, some donations, some for sale to raise funds, and some for the dogs in their care. My car was often filled to the brim with much of the same matter.

"No problem," I said.

Our destination was Captain's Cove Restaurant, back in Sanford. Erica surveyed the older suburban neighborhoods on the route, comprised primarily of single-story 1970s houses with fenceless lawns, with a steely eye.

"I'm always looking for pit bulls," she said. "So many people breed here or just keep their dogs on chains. Happens all the time. It makes me sick."

While I drove around the country, so many times I wondered what was going on in the backyards of the millions of house that flashed by. Was there a dog being mistreated? Bred? Fought? I wanted to know, but then I didn't want to know. My fear was finding a bad situation. I always dealt with it at the time, but I certainly didn't seek it out. Not Erica. She was a warrior on the hunt, ready to take on whomever and whatever crossed her path.

The highway ran alongside Lake Monroe and Erica pointed out something in the distance. "Look, Michelle, do you see that? Those little heads and eyes above the water? Those are alligators."

Sure enough, I could see the beady eyes, the crooked heads, the rough skin. Alligators, lots of them. Dozens.

"Ugh," I said, shuddering. "That totally freaks me out! My best friend growing up came from Florida. She told me that her family would go water skiing in places where there were alligators and poisonous snakes. No way could I do that."

"When Grant was a kid, he and his brother used to go swimming in a hole on their property. They knew there was an alligator in it, so they would take turns being the lookout while the other one swam," she said, looking sideways to gauge my reaction.

I grimaced. "Seriously? That's crazy!"

"Grant once took me out into a swamp, at night, on an air boat. Well, we ran out of gas, so Grant had to jump in the water and pull the boat back in for a few miles."

"No way!"

"Yep. It was winter, so most of the gators were asleep," Erica said, laughing at my shocked face. "You just get used to it out here."

"I don't know if I could ever get used to it," I said, glad to be watching those eerie reptilian faces fade away from the comfort of a moving vehicle. "Grant's pretty bad ass, though, I have to say."

Captain's Cove was a unique place. Inside, the décor was typical seafood restaurant: red leather chairs and dark wood tables with ship wheels, nets, and stuffed fish strewn all over the walls. Outside was something I'd never seen at eating establishment, a large swimming pool where guests swam, then sunned themselves on a patio or strolled up to an outdoor bar for drinks and appetizers. There were a few dogs out there, too, catching some rays. Florida definitely had its charms.

Erica introduced herself to the owners as I began setting up my table alongside some Dolly's Foundation volunteers.

The "Pints for Pits" event cost $10 for a really cool pint glass with Dolly's face on it, plus a beer or soda to fill it up with. Erica also had Dolly's Foundation T-shirts and buttons for sale.

Supporters began to drift in, hugging Erica, many of them giving her status updates about the Dolly's Foundation dogs in their care.

Amos, a stray that suffered severe wounds after being attacked by an alligator at Lake Monroe, had been taken in by Jen and Jason in Jacksonville. The married couple absolutely adored the handsome male pit bull who looked a lot like Dolly.

"Amos had gaping, open wounds. We had to staple and glue him back together at the shelter," Erica told me. "If he didn't look like Dolly's twin, I'm sure he would've been put down."

A woman named Rose came over to greet us. She had agreed to foster Shelby, a five month old tripod who lost a front leg to injury, but quickly became a foster failure, a term applied when the arrangement turned into an adoption.

"A foster failure is the best kind of failure to be," I told Rose, with admiration. "That's awesome."

The Florida humidity was getting to me, even as the sun went down. There was a film of sweat on my chest and face. My hair was pinned up in a bun, but willful tendrils kept escaping. My rather unkempt appearance was nothing like the "Pit Stops" cover. As people came over to buy books and get them signed, I was halfway embarrassed about how bad I looked and half in awe that anyone wanted to read the story. Many of them shared their dog experiences and told me to keep up the great work I was doing.

Me? I thought. They were my heroes. The fosters, the adopters, the ones that did the hard, hands-on work. Sometimes I didn't feel legit, since I didn't foster. Our household limit was two dogs and a cat, a rule thrown down by Wayde. I'd had four dogs when we met in 2005 and handled it fairly well, but it wasn't a lifestyle Wayde wanted, so I acquiesced. By the time we moved in together in 2009, I was down to just Sam and Buster, anyway. Jake and Willy, the older members of my pack, had passed away of natural causes.

Only having two dogs allowed me to volunteer a lot more at Brittany or fundraise or help out at adoption events or write about animal welfare, which I think are my true talents. And since it took a long time for Sam and Buster to gel as a duo, to stop fighting, I felt like bringing another dog in would disrupt the harmony. That's why I didn't adopt Loren and another reason fostering really wasn't in the cards for me.

But still, there were times I'd see a dog in need on Facebook and think to myself, if only. I'd make it work, some crates here, some gates there. Cats on the upper floor, dogs on the lower floors. It was all planned out in my head. Really, the only thing that stopped me from becoming an episode of "Confessions: Animal Hoarding" was Wayde.

***

The Tundra sliced through the dark, muggy night as Erica and I made our way back to Geneva. We were both happy. I had sold quite a few books and Dolly's Foundation had raised a good sum of money, enough to apply for official non-profit status.

"DF just has the best people," Erica said proudly. "When I started this in January, people just came out of the woodwork to help. Now we have this family of supporters. It's very exciting."

"Well, you're pretty awesome, so I'm not surprised this is happening," I told her.

"Thanks. Hey, how's Loren doing?"

"Fantastic. Stefan's the perfect daddy for her. I couldn't have asked for a happier ending for Loren."

"I love it when that happens."

"You know what's weird? Stefan found Loren because of some puppies I had posted on Adopt A Pet, a courtesy listing for a foster that wasn't even a volunteer with Brittany," I told Erica. "We didn't think a puppy would be ideal for Stefan, so we suggested Loren and that was that. You never know how connections are going to be made."

"That's so true," Erica said.

"Do you want to hear a story about those puppies and their mama? It's pretty sad."

## Hello Dolly

Erica nodded.

It wasn't something I shared with everyone.

A woman from Littlerock, a desolate desert town in the Antelope Valley, had contacted Bow-Wows and Meows because she had found a pregnant pit bull and what she assumed was the dog's young son. The situation was turned over to me, the pit lover. I called the woman, named Chris, who spoke with a rapid-fire Spanish accent.

"People out here, they dump dogs all the time. One of my neighbors said she thinks the mama was used for fighting. No one else would take them in. They were going from house to house for days," Chris said. "Finally, I took them home."

She didn't use Facebook or email, nor did Chris own a digital camera, so I asked her to send me photos that I could scan for a fundraising plea for dog food. The photos came a few days later. One was of a crop-eared, scarred, heavily pregnant female, the other of a floppy-eared, bright-eyed youngster who looked to be about four or five months old. Both were white with black spots. Chris had named the mom Zephyr and the son Sinbad.

Some very generous friends pitched in, including Tim and Jessica of Margo's Bark, so I was able to bring Chris and the dogs $300 worth of food a week later. Zephyr had since had her pups. I was anxious to meet and get photos of everyone to start networking.

Her house was modest and the Toyota minivan Chris drove was ancient. Chris worked as a senior home caregiver in Santa Clarita and didn't make much money, so taking on these dogs was not easy for her. She was also something of hoarder, I came to find out. She had 10 cats living in one room, plus five dogs (four chow/shepherd mixes and a Chihuahua) that she kept separated from Zephyr, Sinbad and the remaining five pups. Eight of the original 13 had died.

"I planted them in the yard. I cried with each and every one," Chris told me. "It broke my heart."

The biggest shock of all was Sinbad. He wasn't the small pup from the photo. He was practically a full-grown adult, about 75 pounds, with a huge head and the most adorable black spot over his eye. How long had Chris really had these dogs? Why didn't she ask for help sooner? I was growing angry, but kept it to myself. At least Chris didn't take them to the Lancaster shelter, where all the dogs surely would've been killed.

The situation seemed pretty untenable, since Chris lived alone and didn't have any help with her very large pack. I expressed my concerns.

"It's OK," Chris assured me. "I let them out a group at a time. Sinbad's OK with most of my dogs, it's Zephyr that doesn't want anyone around her or the puppies. I keep them separate."

"Please be careful," I implored, hoping for the best, but knowing that this situation could go bad at any time.

I took new photos of Sinbad, Zephyr and the pups and posted them on Facebook, keeping in touch with Chris for updates on everyone's condition.

One day, several weeks later, I received a frantic call.

"Oh my God, Michelle," said a crying Chris. She pronounced my name Me-shell. "Michelle, something horrible happened. Just horrible. Oh my God."

"Chris, calm down. Take a deep breath. What's wrong? Tell me."

She had come home from work to let Zephyr and the pups out into the backyard. Somehow, her original pack of five opened the bedroom window and scrambled down the stucco siding to the yard. As her chow mix Honey approached one of the puppies, Zephyr snapped and attacked her. A hysterical Chris was screaming and trying to break up the fight, when a neighbor looked over the wall that separated their yards. Moments later, the neighbor came back with a rope.

"Use this, put it around the pit's neck and pull them apart," the neighbor instructed Chris.

Desperate, Chris did so and Zephyr was yanked against the wall. She began to pick up her dog Honey, who was bleeding profusely from several puncture wounds, then looked at her neighbor.

"Go ahead and take care of her," the neighbor told Chris.

She took the dying Honey into her bathroom. Sobbing, Chris applied towels to try and stop the bleeding, to little avail. She stayed with Honey for quite some time before remembering to check on Zephyr.

There, against the wall, in a sit position, was Zephyr. She was dead, choked by the rope at the hands of her neighbors.

"You killed her!" Chris said, rushing over to free Zephyr. "How could you? You were just supposed to hold her back."

"We didn't kill her. She just died. She must have had a heart attack," the male neighbor said.

## Hello Dolly

"No, she didn't. You killed her!"

As Chris wailed about Zephyr, the neighbor told her, "Now you need to get rid of that other pit bull, too, or we're going to call Animal Control on you. You have until tomorrow morning."

Chris first took Honey to a vet, where she died. Distraught, now Chris had to find a place for Sinbad or risk his life by surrendering him to the shelter.

"I don't know what to do, Michelle. It's all so horrible," Chris said, once again starting to sob.

My mind spun, but I was determined to at least help Sinbad get out of this mess alive. "I'll see if Brittany Foundation can take Sinbad. Let me see what I can do. Please, just hold on until I find out more."

I placed a call to Rene Ruston, the board member who had the most pull with Nancy, and explained the situation. Within minutes, the reply came. Sinbad was in. I called Chris and gave her directions. While grateful to Brittany Foundation for taking Sinbad at the last minute, it was not a trip Chris really wanted to make. She called me that night.

"Sinbad was so confused, Michelle, he just cried for me when I left," Chris said, almost hysterical before breaking into low muffled sobs. "It's all just so awful."

"It is, Chris. I'm so sorry. But Sinbad is safe and he will be well taken care of. We'll find him a home. You take care of those puppies and we'll find them families, too."

The second order of business was getting Sinbad a new name. Sinbad was too old-school for most people to remember its origin and even if they did, was it great for a dog to be named after a somewhat forgettable Greek myth or a B-list comedian? Plus, it was a double negative and pits had a hard enough time as it was. He needed a happy, popular name. Since "Twilight" was all the rage, I thought we should christen him Edward or Jacob. He definitely seemed more macho than the wimpy Edward, so Jake it was. Whether it was the name or his charm or both, Jake was only in rescue a few months before Ashlyn adopted him.

To Chris' credit, and through the help of AngelDogs Foundation, a mobile spay/neuter clinic that hosted low-cost clinics in Littlerock once a month, the rest of the puppies were fixed. Three of the puppies were adopted shortly thereafter into great homes, one with Stefan's friends Randy and Brooke, who were looking for a pal for their pit EZ. They took a girl, black and white like her brother Jake, and named her Squats.

Chris kept the other two puppies. Rene told me to cut her off from dog food if she wouldn't give them up. "Chris is a hoarder and you can't reward that behavior," she said.

Though I worried about the animal's welfare, I listened to Rene. She was right. I told Chris as diplomatically as possible that it was a bad idea to keep them, that it was harder to adopt out older pit bulls than puppies, that her neighbor could snap at any time and insist she take them to the shelter. Chris still wouldn't budge, even when I offered to find them homes. We hadn't spoken since.

"So, as far as I know, she still has all those dogs," I concluded the story. "Sad, huh?"

I looked over at Erica. Her eyes were fixed in a flinty stare, her hands clutched hard on the steering wheel. "Why didn't anyone call the police on the neighbors? It's not right. They should be in jail for killing that dog," she said in a low, throaty voice.

"Erica, what would happen then? Chris had way too many animals. All of them would've gone to the shelter and probably be killed."

She took in a deep breath and slowly exhaled. "I know, but it sucks. Those bastards should have to pay somehow," Erica said in a low voice. "It's always the pits that suffer. Those bastards. I wish I could get my hands on them."

From the look on Erica's face, I had a feeling that was a fight those dog killers would lose.

# The Low Country

Moss dripped off the ancient trees that canopied the two-lane highway. Sweat dripped off my forehead as I took Kara out for a potty break. We were in South Carolina, the low country, to go camping. Yes, camping. I hadn't given up just yet.

This time, though, we scored a spot within walking distance of the beach and where, I was told, there were no gators. Just the occasional non-poisonous snake. Hunting Island Park itself is shaded, its sites lined with tall trees and overrun with kids on bicycles. It was Memorial Day Weekend and the place was packed at 5 p.m. I was comforted by the tent to RV ratio, as well as our close proximity to the clean restroom.

Some of my neighbors' tents were amazing, two-bedroom models with enclosed canopies. I set up our little dome quickly, despite the

*"No gators here, Aunt Michelle!"*

incredible humidity. Kara and I headed to the beach briefly, me marveling at the silver and gold flecks imbuing the softly crashing waves, Kara looking every which way at the new landscape. Was it her first time at a beach? She scampered by my side, staying away from the incoming water, while I reveled in its soft coolness.

"Got it!"

Hoping to beat the crowds, we awoke early and hit the beach by 8 a.m. There was a long stretch of sand, surrounded by sea oats and tide pools, with no one around. I smiled and took out a tennis ball. I threw it and Kara jetted down the beach, kicking up sand in her path. After a few long treks, she was panting.

To cool down, I gently led Kara into the scattered tide pools, some clear enough to see tiny little fish swimming around. Kerplunk. She went in, almost up to her chest in spots as the pools deceptively dropped, looking up to me for reassurance. It wasn't long before Kara scrambled out, shaking off the water as the sun glistened on her wet golden fur.

We resumed our game of fetch on the cool, damp sand. I threw the ball, closer and closer to the waves and Kara went right after it. I laughed when she skid and rolled onto her side or even completely around, returning with a hanging, panting tongue and sand on her snout.

"Again?" Kara silently asked me and obligingly I continued, enjoying the sun and the perfect moment, until both of us were spent. We tried to nap in our stuffy, steamy little tent, but it was impossible for either of us to get comfortable. So I carried Kara into the car and sat with her for two hours, cranking up the A/C and listening to the Rolling Stones while reading. It was the least I could do for my little friend, who was quite content to sprawl on her pink blanket and snooze the afternoon away.

Lunch that day was at the Shrimp Shack for a shrimp salad. This was shrimp country, after all. That night, I enjoyed one of my favorite meals ever, a shrimp boil bursting with the succulent shellfish, potatoes, onions and corn, dipped into melted butter. Since coming to the south, like Bubba in "Forrest Gump," I'd had shrimp etouffee, fried shrimp, shrimp po boy, shrimp salad, shrimp boil, you name it...I ate it...and I loved it.

***

Though our camping experience was finally a pleasant one, it was still wonderful to check into the La Quinta in Raleigh, which was the nicest room we'd had up to that point. Appointed with a mile-long desk, flat screen TV, mini-fridge and a huge king size bed, along with colorful artwork and a nice view of the trees outside, it was like having a studio apartment to ourselves.

I decided to find the spot of the next signing in advance so I wouldn't be late the following day.

*"Sweet!"*

Phydeaux Raleigh was one of the coolest pet stores I've ever seen, a 14,000 square foot loft-style space with everything you could ever want for your four-legged friend. I brought Kara in with me and introduced us to the manager. While we picked up some dog food for her, as well as a couple of new balls, I had started thinking about supper for me.

I'm not usually much of a pizza fan, but I had seen a rather cool-looking pizza joint down the street and asked the staff about it. A light dinner sounded good after consuming pounds of shrimp in the days before. "Best pizza in town," I was told. "Great salads, too."

Lilly's Pizza had hipster written all over it. Outside on the patio, tattooed and pierced rockers mingled with intentionally geeky collegiate types. Rock and roll was blaring inside the industrial space. The menu was intriguing, featuring the thin crust I always preferred with a multitude of toppings, many vegetarian. I decided to build my own with a decadent white sauce as the base, topped with lots of garlic and tomato, accompanied by a vegetarian antipasto salad.

Kara sniffed the air when I returned, but didn't try to ransack my dinner. I really appreciated her restraint. My black lab Jake had been the type of food hound that wouldn't relent until I gave him a piece of whatever I was eating. It made traveling with him a challenge.

We hurried back into the hotel and as I went to prepare Kara's food, I realized the canned food I bought at Phydeaux did not have a pop top. It required an opener, which I didn't have.

I called the front desk. They didn't have one either. My blood started to boil. This required a trip out again, which was not easy, considering we were in the heart of a busy intersection and needed to make a U-turn that took about 10 minutes. The food was going to get cold and I was hungry.

Kara looked at me quizzically as I stomped around, cursing. There's a saying "It's not the elephant in the living room, but the ants in the kitchen that'll make you crazy," that I definitely relate to. Hand me an emergency and I'll handle it with aplomb, but inconvenience me when I'm hungry and tired and I can be a real baby, at least when it's only a dog that'll witness my tantrum.

The gas station convenience store a mile away from the hotel took us 15 minutes to access. As I huffily made my way inside, I noticed a homeless man who had taken off his shoes and was rubbing his feet.

I took a deep breath and exhaled, feeling like a petty asshole for my quality problems. After my purchase, I headed over and handed him $3, enough to buy a drink and a snack, anyway.

"God bless you," he said with a big smile.

"Same to you," I said, wishing I could do more. Homeless people touched my heart almost as much as homeless pets and if they had a dog, forget it. That combo could always be counted on for a donation from me – usually dog food and a few bucks. Would the money be used for alcohol or something I didn't consider necessary? Who knows. Sometimes you just had to trust.

Kara and I ate dinner together, she with her kibble mixed with wet food, me with a satisfyingly crisp crusted pizza and a very fresh, savory mix of greens. Afterwards, we settled on the bed, grateful for the softness of that mattress, a Godsend after 400 miles on the road. Soon enough, both of us were snoring.

***

The next night, we met with Carolina Care Bullies for the book signing. The non-profit rescue and advocacy organization has a wide foster network that saves bully breeds from shelters or other untenable situations.

Rae Boney and her boyfriend JR were setting up the event at Phydeaux with Rae's 8-year old son Sebastion. They brought along their foster Lilo, a gorgeous young brindle girl. Rae was a ray of sunshine, with her curly strawberry blonde hair and vibrant nature.

The trio had started fostering for CCB only a few months before taking in two bully puppy brothers, Ben and Aaron, on Superbowl Sunday. Ben found a home right away, so they brought Lilo in. Both were still awaiting homes.

Rae looked proudly at her son, who was petting Kara. "Sebastion really likes the dogs. Sometimes he gets frustrated at the extra chores, but he comes to almost all the events with me," she said. "Anytime we do an event, and there are children with parents, I'll look over and Sebastion's talking to the kids. He's just got a great little personality."

After some quality time with Sebastion, Kara made herself right at home with Lilo, playing gently at first, then laying right by her side.

Chipmunk, a handsome little brown and white boy, also joined the group, as did Willow, a black beauty.

Attendance was light for the signing, mostly just the volunteers and their dogs. It was a weeknight, so I wasn't too surprised, but it was disappointing. My inventory of books was moving slowly and my goal of selling them all before returning to California was looking ever more remote. Still, we enjoyed the camaraderie of the dogs and their foster parents, learning each story and retelling our own.

*"Have you met my friend Lilo? She's looking for a home..."*

# The Low Country

In the last half hour or so, a tall, pretty brunette walked in and looked me straight in the eye. She looked vaguely familiar, but I couldn't place the face.

"Are you here for the signing?" I asked, curious.

"Yes, I'm here to see you. I'm Ashley Trexler," she replied.

"Oh my God!" I screamed and gave her a big hug.

Ashley is the daughter of Mark and Julie Trexler, whom Loren and I visited in Dublin, Georgia. I hadn't seen Ashley since she was about 12, which was more than 15 years ago. Our families would go camping and vacationing at Leo Carrillo Beach and Bass Lake together. Ashley was such a sweet young girl and she'd grown up into a beautiful woman.

Since Ashley worked in Raleigh as a technical customer support representative, she stopped by to say hi to me. We ended up having dinner at the Sunflower Café just down the street. Though the patio wasn't inherently dog-friendly, they made an exception for Kara. I placed her on top of a small table, while Ashley lifted her down onto the patio, since there was no entry gate.

Kara just sat on the shaded concrete, enjoying a bowl of ice water and the evening air, which was growing increasingly, welcomingly cool, getting excited only when a squirrel would bound by on its way to a tree. Café life suited her.

Ashley had the shrimp and grits, while I, for a change of pace, had the grilled grouper, a firm whitefish with a delectable lemon-infused cream sauce, rice and sautéed spinach with garlic. Heaven. Kara had a grilled, cut up chicken breast, which she happily wolfed down, then assumed the platypus pose.

Satisfied, the three of us whiled away the warm summer evening until the sun started going down. Ashley inquired about Loren.

"She's doing fantastic. Stefan just adores her. He's trained her to get along with other dogs and everything," I told Ashley, a big smile on my face. "Loren totally scored."

"That's great. My parents were seriously considering adopting her, if she hadn't found a home," Ashley said. "They travel a lot, but my mom said she would've made it work."

"Really? That's so cool. I didn't know that," I said, reaching down and patting Kara on the head. "Let's hope Kara has the same happy ending Loren did."

Kara looked up at me adoringly. No matter what, I knew she was safe with Kyle. That gave me comfort, though I knew I'd still cry when it was time to return her. It was inevitable. I would be losing my new best friend.

# B-Town

Leaving for Baltimore was not auspicious. Excited and nervous about our signing that night, which promised to be our biggest to date, I had slept about three hours. It didn't help that Kara had to pee at three in the morning, either. As she did her business, a 1970s burnt orange Cadillac, jacked up three feet high on pneumatic shocks, slowly cruised the parking lot, hip hop blaring, bass thumping. My heart pounded in my chest along to the music.

"Hurry up, Kara," I said nervously, tugging on her leash. She looked up at me briefly, then continued to sniff around for the perfect spot to pee.

The car parked, its engine revving. OMG. Was this a gang retaliation, the proverbial drive by? Was the driver looking for someone in the hotel? What the hell did he think of this crazy middle-aged woman, hair all puffed up from southern humidity, dressed in sloppy sweats with a stout little pit bull at her side at this time of night?

All this rang through my head as we casually, or so I hoped, walked back to our room, purposely not looking in the car's direction. As we neared the door, the car backed out of the spot and left. I exhaled sharply.

So, needless to say, when my GPS died at 8 in the morning as we tried to make our way to Baltimore, I was more than a little upset. Downloading a navigator app to my Blackberry met with no success. It kept saying I was out of GPS signal.

"I'm in the middle of a major city in America. What do you mean I have no GPS? You suck!" I screamed at the phone. Kara looked at me, shock and concern registering on her usually tranquil face. Yes, there was nothing like yelling at inanimate objects to make one feel truly stupid, but I was desperate. I have absolutely no sense of direction, so scouring the Atlas in my car only served to heighten my frustration.

Since it was 5 a.m. in California and I knew Wayde wasn't awake yet, there was only one place to call. My father in Idaho Falls, whom I knew would be up and already on his computer. We called him the human compass, a gene he did not pass down to his daughter.

He picked it up on the second ring. "Hey, Mich, how's it going?"

The poor man did not know what he was in for. I was in full meltdown mode.

"Not good. I'm lost, my GPS is broken, I'm going to be late to Baltimore, I've had no sleep," I said, barely taking a breath in between complaints and tears.

"Aww, Mich..." Pops started, but I cut him off.

"What the hell am I doing anyway?" I was alternating between crying and yelling now. "Real authors don't do crap like this. I am a self-published joke. I'll never get anywhere. I don't know what I was thinking! I should just go home!"

"Sweetie, calm down. You're not a joke. Just take a deep breath. We'll get you on the right track."

Sure enough, Pops started me on the path towards Baltimore, and miraculously, the navigator app sprang to life about 10 minutes in. The GPS said we should arrive in Baltimore by 2 p.m., which left us plenty of time to check in, take a shower and meet Jen Carle, rescuer extraordinaire and one of our book tour sponsors.

Jen was another Facebook friend and fellow author of the charming dog books "Becoming Waldo" and "Finally Winsome," based on her own experiences with rescue and dog ownership. She was avid supporter of Baltimore Animal Rescue and Care Shelter, personally advocating for hard-luck pit bulls, such as Windsor the bait dog, often paying for their boarding and medical care until they got adopted or rescued. Jen had also lobbied hard for Ava, a beautiful white pit bull that had been sexually abused by a teenage boy, to get a second chance. Ultimately, Best Friends took Ava, much to Jen's relief.

Raven, a tan and white pit bull from BARCS, made her way into Jen's pack after she was slated to be euthanized due to a severely injured leg. Jen stepped into foster Raven, paid for her medical bills and adopted her shortly thereafter, naming the dog after her favorite football team. Her loyalty to the Baltimore Ravens was never-ending, second only to helping dogs.

Jen and I were set to do a triple signing for a BARCS fundraiser at a chic downtown Mexican restaurant at 5:30 along with Pamela Black

Townsend, a photographer, rescuer and author of "Black is Beautiful: A Celebration of Dark Dogs."

My friend Christelle Del Prete, a rescuer and animal welfare writer from Bridgewater, Massachusetts, was coming too, with her newly adopted pit mix Rusty. Christelle and I originally met on the first Pit Stops trip, over lunch at Whole Foods with Loren in Connecticut.

Problem was, traffic was not cooperating, stalling completely in several places, including the dreaded Washington loop. Though it was cool to see the Pentagon and several other landmarks, my heart sank every time I put on the brakes. My mind spun. I had not taken a shower. I was exhausted. I looked horrible. I was going to be a dirty, incoherent idiot at what promised to be our biggest event to date. It was enough to make me cry. Repeatedly. (As I got older, I found my emotions more and more difficult to control. Could it be hormones? Was I really middle-aged?)

Kara took all of it in stride, snoozing softly in the comfort of the air-conditioned car. When some idiot cut me off, nearly causing me to crash and sending Kara flying to the floorboard, she just shook it off and calmly climbed back up to her pink-blanketed perch.

"I'm so sorry, Kare Bear," I said, patting her rump. She closed her eyes and went back to sleep. I continued stroking her tawny fur as a form of stress relief.

Meanwhile, through a series of frantic phone calls, I found out that Christelle was having the same problem on her end. Neither of us would make it before 4 p.m., if we were lucky. I called Jen in a panic. She was picking us up for the event, thank God. I was too much of a wreck to drive any more.

"No problem," she said in a cheerful voice. "Just take your time and be safe. I'll pick you up around 5 p.m. in the lobby."

"I'm sorry to be such a spaz, to whine to you when we've never even met before," I told Jen.

"Well, I consider you a friend. Don't even worry about it."

Hanging up, I managed a half-smile. As crazy as my life felt on this trip, I was truly blessed to be surrounded by such caring people and Kara, my faithful four-legged buddy.

\*\*\*

We made it to the Sheraton at 4:15 p.m. There was a long grassy walkway, so I took Kara for a potty break before checking in. As we did, the clerk handed me a beautiful bouquet of daisies and a gift bag with tasty goodies for me and Kara. "Welcome to Baltimore!" the handwritten note said. Of course, it was from Jen. The kind gesture brought tears of gratitude. This woman was the soul of hospitality.

On the elevator, Kara and I were surrounded by a congregation of Africans there for a convention. Dressed in colorful garb, several of the women gave a little "Ooh" and scooted out of Kara's way, looking scared. In this case, I didn't think it was pit bull prejudice, but probably a cultural fear of dogs, so I let it slide. I did offer a quiet, "She's friendly," which seemed to fall on deaf ears.

I took a fast shower, fed Kara and tried to make myself presentable. Jen and Christelle were waiting in the lobby with Rusty, a handsome white and orange dog whose tail wagged nonstop as soon as he saw Kara. Their introduction went swimmingly and quick hugs went all around for the humans, too.

I felt slightly delirious as we sped away in Jen's large SUV, Kara and I sequestered away in the cavernous back row. Jen's pretty blonde hair swung about her shoulders as she expertly changed lanes and navigated the chaotic city traffic, simultaneously keeping up a conversation with the two frazzled strangers and curious canines in her car.

We arrived at our destination at 6:15 p.m. We were supposed to be there at 5:30 p.m.

"Oh, well," Jen said with a royal wave of her hand. "Fashionably late. We're the famous authors. They'll just have to wait for us."

The scene at Miguel's was lively, with people mingling and enjoying cocktails. The modern concrete structure had several low-slung couches scattered about the huge, open patio. Kara immediately made herself comfortable after being admired by Ashley Ferrell, a BARCS kennel attendant. Shortly thereafter, Kara was on Ashley's lap for most of the evening, while Jen, Pam and I met with dog lovers, volunteers and advocates.

The mayor of Baltimore even came out. A BARCS supporter bought her a copy of "Pit Stops," which I was happy to autograph, especially after the mayor's husband told Christelle and I about the pregnant pit bull named Olive he and his wife had fostered.

In the morning, bolstered by a great night's sleep on an incredibly soft mattress, Kara and I played a rousing game of fetch on a hidden patch of grass at the hotel. Christelle and Rusty met us at 10 a.m. in the lobby.

Jen was going to watch Kara and Rusty for us while we toured Baltimore Animal Rescue and Care Shelter. Christelle planned on writing a story about BARCS for the Best Friends website, while I was writing one for the blog. Jen, or Aunt Jen, had boarded her own dogs so Rusty and Kara could have the run of the place, an incredibly kind gesture.

"Are you kidding? This is going to be as fun for me as it is for them," Jen told us.

The dogs skid around happily on Jen's hardwood floors and Kara was in heaven when she went outside to a large, fenced backyard full of toys.

"Catch, Kara!" Jen said and threw a bright neon ball. Kara immediately set off after the inanimate prey, doing a roly poly that made us all giggle, then brought the ball back to Jen, her new best friend.

"Be careful, Jen. You'll be doing this all day," I warned her.

"I don't mind. We're going to have fun!" Jen proclaimed, throwing the ball again. This time Rusty joined in, but Kara was too quick.

I had no doubt the trio would have a blast. Christelle and I, however, were anticipating a rather harsh shelter experience, having been forewarned by a few of the volunteers beforehand that BARCS was dreary and in dire need of updating.

Actually, BARCS wasn't bad at all. The building itself was old, but the reception area was bright and welcoming, plastered with colorful posters announcing upcoming events. There were several volunteers walking dogs, many we had met the night before. Others were putting together doggy play groups in a large outdoor run.

Jennifer Brause greeted us in her office. Brause, who originally acted as a consultant to BARCS in 2004, was running the facility just a year later. The only open door facility in Baltimore, BARCS takes in more than 30 homeless animals a day and houses up to 400 at a time.

"When I started, the euthanasia rate was 98 percent. The focus was on enforcement, not on adoption. Now we're down to a 38 percent euthanasia rate," Jennifer said.

There was a mix of 50 percent dogs to cats at BARCS, though the dog situation was usually more dramatic. "We get a lot of backyard breeders and backyard fighting dogs, sometimes in groups of six or more. We see this weekly," Jennifer said.

That means pits make up the majority of the dog population, sometimes up to the 90 percent range. Ashley, whom we met the night before, toured us through three of six dog kennel areas, which were painted a cheerful yellow and in the process of being cleaned by staff. At 19, Ashley was studying to become a vet tech and had written her college term paper on pit bulls. She was a very mature, astute young woman.

Ashley introduced us to each dog by name and gave us their back story. There was Mama, a breeding dog with scars. Sweet Pepper, suffering silently in the corner of her kennel from a severe flea allergy. Mork, brought in with his sister Mindy, who got adopted. He was still waiting for his forever home.

"People like flashy, high-contrast, blue and fawn pits, so black or plain dogs often get overlooked," Ashley said sadly. "Half of the people don't want pit bulls, but the kennel staff knows the breed and loves them, so we try to educate potential

*Ashley Ferrell and a canine friend at BARCS*

adopters."

The staff also bonds together to save dogs that have been at BARCS for a while, working on any behavioral issues, crossposting on Facebook and connecting with rescue groups. Known as the BARCS Pit Crew, the group goes the extra mile with their favorite breed, getting professional photographs taken, and taking to the dogs to advocacy and education events for additional exposure.

What struck me while touring BARCS was not the institutional surroundings, it was the love the staff had for these dogs. Each was held, cuddled, acknowledged and praised while the kennels were cleaned. They were treated, if for a few brief moments, as if they were wanted, as if they were a family pet.

It seemed the staff enjoyed it as much as the dogs. "We get lots of hugs and kisses here on a daily basis," Ashley said cheerfully.

*** 

By night, Eric Vocke of Baltimore Bully Crew was a chef at the Pierpoint Inn, a charming, intimate bistro in the heart of the city. By day, Eric was a crusader for the pit bulls in his hometown. A friend of Jen's, Eric was known for his hardcore advocacy, as well as incredible smoked crab cakes. He agreed to a lunchtime interview with me and Christelle. After BARCS, we made our way to the Pierpoint Inn.

While cooking a crab cake for me and a spicy noodle curry dish for vegetarian Christelle, a delivery man came in and struck up a conversation with Eric. This was prompted by Eric's distinctive black Baltimore Bully Crew T-shirt, which had "Fight Abuse Not Dogs" emblazoned on the back. The $20 shirts are BBC's primary fundraising tool. Other sayings include "Dog Fighters Are Bitches."

"Yeah, I've heard of some guys who file their dog's teeth into points before a fight," the dreadlocked delivery man told Eric as Christelle and I listened on, shocked.

These types of anecdotes don't faze Eric anymore. He's spent years studying and researching dog fighting, soaking up the lingo and absorbing the culture to make inroads into ghettos surrounding Baltimore. "Before fights, some guys will sharpen the dog's teeth with a Dremel and shoot them up with cocaine to numb the pain. In one case, a dog's teeth were ripped out with hangers," Eric said as Christelle and

I inhaled our lunch. "Money is the number one drive, but fighters also live vicariously through these dogs. There's a sense of strength they get about possessing an animal and being able to make it violent on command. They manipulate everything that's good about pit bulls."

While I was absorbed in the conversation, which should have turned my stomach, I silently wondered how I could ask for another crab cake without being rude. It was so delicious and though I may look small, I have a big appetite. I just didn't have the heart to interrupt Eric, who was speaking with machine-gun rapidity about his rather intense experiences.

"There's so much dog fighting in Baltimore, on street corners, with the hustlers. If the dog is lucky, it will go to BARCS," he told us.

When a dog is not so lucky, Eric and his wife Kate, plus ten or so friends who make up the Baltimore Bully Crew, will often go to the alleys, the abandoned buildings and other places where bait dogs and losing fight dogs are found dumped or chained. The first dog BBC rescued just over a year prior was chained to an abandoned building with a signed stapled to her flesh stating, "I'm a fighting dog who won't fight, I'm useless."

"It was all misspelled, of course," Eric said.

The dog came to be known as Mozzarella. "I like to give pit bulls silly food names. It makes them less intimidating," he said. Other BBC alumni include Pork Chop and Sugar Snap.

Mozzarella came to live with the Vockes and Eric slept with her for 72 nights straight. The BBC rehabilitates dogs like Mozzarella, restoring not only their health, but their confidence, before finding the proper pit-savvy forever homes. "It's a one dog at a time approach," Eric said. "We've had up to 15, but we prefer having three or four at a time."

In addition to rescue, Eric also gives talks to the residents of local juvenile detention centers about dog fighting, showing gruesome videos to illustrate his point. Once, during a presentation, an 11 year old boy stood up and told Eric, "Man, your shit is weak. I can go to the alley behind my house and see a better fight than that any day of the week."

Eric sighed and was quiet for a split second as Christelle and I shook our heads in disbelief. "That's why we need to get these kids when they're six or seven years old, before they start looking up to their older brothers who dog fight."

After lunch, Eric drove us through a tough neighborhood in Baltimore, just a few blocks from the restaurant, to illustrate his point. He honked and stuck his head outside the window of his ancient red Honda Civic, adorned with anti-dog fighting stickers, pointing and shouting things like, "People fight dogs in this park all the time."

From the comfort of the RAV4, Christelle and I surveyed the scene, a grim urban landscape of battered apartment buildings with barred and broken windows scattered amongst liquor stores and laundromats.

"Wow, Eric's a brave guy," Christelle said, a hint of awe in her voice.

"Yeah, he's pretty gnarly," I said, equally impressed.

Eric led us back to his more suburban neighborhood a few miles away, not too far from Jen's house, where Kate and their dog Peyton

*Eric and Kate Vocke of Baltimore Bully Crew with their dog Peyton*

waited in a greenbelt.

Peyton, a strong, striking brown and white pit with big ears like Kara's, was instantly thrilled to see his daddy. A former bait dog, Peyton was one of the lucky few to call the Vockes family.

When I asked why Peyton got this honor over the many dogs BBC rescues, Eric got teary-eyed, which he tended to do when discussing the dogs he's rehabilitated.

"He was only 29 pounds when we found him. Peyton was in such bad shape, half his ear fell off in Kate's hand," Eric said. "He needed us the most."

\*\*\*

Over at Jen's, the canine campers were exhausted after a day of playing ball, belly rubs and tasty snacks. So much so, that Kara and Rusty barely awoke from their naps upon our arrival. Jen had to call them over. Kara yawned and sauntered over to greet me, while Rusty bounded to Christelle once he was aware of his mom's return.

"How were they?" I asked, smooshing Kara's jowls and leaning in for a smooch, which she quickly granted.

"They were great," Jen said. "I'm going to miss them."

"I'm sure they'll miss you, too," Christelle said. "They probably want to stay here forever!"

The five of us gathered on Jen's expansive front lawn as I took pictures. Jen rolled around the grass with Kara, bestowing kiss after kiss on her big head and silly mouth, saying goodbye as only pit lovers do. Kara was enthralled and Jen had a huge grin on her face. She was now officially Aunt Jen.

Snapping away, the thought came to me that at this moment, while Kara was being loved and adored, there must be hundreds, if not thousands, of pit bulls in dark basements, chained in a yard or getting prepared to fight within just a few square miles of this idyllic scene. My eyes started to well up. I was happy for Kara, but sad, too, saying a silent prayer for the dogs who weren't so lucky.

# B-Town

*"Aunt Jen is the best!"*

*"Aw, do we really have to go?"*

## Buckets O' Fun

Compared to Baltimore, the 250 mile drive to Pittsburgh was super serene. Easy like Sunday morning, as the Commodores used to sing. We were going to stay with Rebecca Courtad and her family in Morgan, just outside the city, for a few days in between signings with Hello Bully and Western Pennsylvania Humane Society.

Rebecca and I met online during the first Pit Stops outing. She was one of the first people to donate to me and Loren's adventure and held a special place in my heart. Though we had never met in person, like Jen, Rebecca instantly felt like a good friend.

The cityscape of high rises and condos gave way to hilly, rustic homes with fluffy, emerald green lawns as we drew closer to the Courtad residence. It kind of reminded me of Topanga Canyon back in California, minus the hippy, beachy ambiance.

"I think we're going to like it here, Kare Bear," I said, patting my passenger's rump. She lifted one eye briefly and promptly went back to her slumbering state. Must be nice.

Kara perked up once I slowed the car down to pull up into the Courtad driveway, her ears on high alert. Rebecca was wearing the Pit Stops T-shirt I had sent a few weeks before, a small that fit her perfectly. Though Rebecca was in her early 50s, she looked at least a decade younger. Her hair was full and tousled, while her body was as tanned and toned as a personal trainer.

She sprinted over and welcomed us both with a big hug. "It's so nice to meet you finally," Rebecca said.

"I know," I said, happily returning the embrace. "It's about time, huh?"

Rebecca slung her arm around my shoulder as she introduced her husband Mike and showed us around. There was a sparkling pool surrounded by a covered patio with a gourmet barbecue and bar area. Pop music played and comfortable, overstuffed outdoor furniture beckoned. It made me want to strip down to a bathing suit, get a good book, then take a nap, but we had a signing with Hello Bully in just a few hours. The fantasy would have to wait until tomorrow.

# Buckets O' Fun

Of course, Kara's interest was piqued by the endless, unfenced acreage the Courtad's called their backyard. I suppose when one naps 20 hours a day or more, conjuring up energy on a dime was pretty easy.

"Hey Kara," Mike said, picking a ball off the lawn and holding up in the air.

Immediately, Kara went into attentive soldier pose, not taking her eyes off the prize. Poor Mike was suckered in by her routine, throwing the ball dozens of times as Kara scurried off to catch it. Several times, she was in champion mode, jumping high and catching the ball mid-air, eliciting cheers from her new fan club.

*"What's that in your hand?"*

"Kara's going to love it here," I told Rebecca. "It's going to be endless fetch!"

A small, white fluffy dog came scurrying out to check on the commotion. "That's Riley, my little old man. He's blind and kind of stinky," Rebecca said with affection, reaching down to pat Riley.

Kara trotted over to Riley, sniffed him for a few seconds, then went back to Mike for more fetch.

"Where are your other dogs?" I asked.

"Oh, I boarded them," she said casually.

"Wow, you didn't have to do that."

"I wanted Kara to have the run of the place."

I shook my head. "That is so kind. That you would do that for a couple of strangers…"

"You're not a stranger to me. We're friends."

"Thanks, Rebecca. I already feel right at home. Kara does, too."

Inside, the large, open, ranch-style house featured huge windows and a charming mix of warm Tuscan and country décor. There were a dozen dog toys strewn about the kitchen.

# Pit Stops 2

"Those are for you to play with, Kara," Rebecca said. Kara immediately obliged, gently picking up a plush squeaky and thrashing her head in glee. She trotted along as Rebecca showed us to our room, which featured a heavenly looking queen bed topped with a ton of pillows and a cushy comforter.

"Who's room is this?" I asked.

"Oh, it's Tyler. He's coming home tonight from a trip, but I told him I gave his room away."

"Seriously? Are you sure?"

"I'm sure. He can sleep on the couch or with the other guys downstairs. There's always a slumber party going on here."

Sure enough, the Courtad's younger son Tanner and his friends, mostly neighbors, streamed in and out of the house throughout the afternoon, rifling through the fridge or jumping into the pool. All were incredibly good-looking, like something out of an Abercrombie & Fitch ad. Not surprisingly, Tanner and Brooke, the Courtad's daughter and youngest child, were actual models while Tyler resembled a young Mark Ruffalo.

"Is there something in the water around here? All the kids are gorgeous!" I told Rebecca. "Well, you're stunning, so it's not a big surprise that your kids are too."

"You're too sweet," Rebecca said, waving the compliment away. I had a feeling she deflected this kind of attention a lot.

Reluctant to leave our new digs, yet excited to reunite with my friends from Hello Bully, I got ready quickly and indulged Kara in one last game of fetch before our signing at Quaker Steak & Lube. The restaurant's claim to fame was chicken wings, the thought of which tortured the newly meat-free me.

Wings, when done right, were one of the best things on the planet. There was a wing place in Santa Clarita called Saucey's that I used to be a frequent diner at, indulging in the demi-glace wings and white cheddar fries at least once a week. I literally cried when they went out of business. Could I restrain myself at this wing haven? It was the biggest culinary road temptation to date.

Our set up was on the enclosed patio. I lugged my table and books over, as several Hello Bully volunteers that I had not met before, including event coordinator Nicole Garritano Meloy, came over to meet us or should I say, Kara.

Everyone instantly fell in love with her. I basically handed over the leash and didn't have to worry about Kara for the remainder of the event. She was content to cuddle and charm the crowd, which Kara did effortlessly.

About 15 minutes later, Daisy Balawejder and Amy Dengler came in.

Flashes of our time on the patio at the Doublewide Diner with Loren flashed before me. They hadn't changed a bit. I felt a big grin breaking out.

*"So much love, so little time..."*

"Hey," Daisy called out to me. "Welcome back."

"Hey," I said and pulled her in for a bear hug. "Nice to be back."

Amy tentatively embraced me. "Wow, you're one of the lucky ones," Daisy said with a laugh. "Amy isn't usually a hugger."

"Yeah, well, she came a long way," Amy said. "I'll make an exception."

Daisy looked over at Kara, who had made herself very comfortable in a young woman's lap. The volunteer was sitting on the concrete floor to accommodate Kara.

"She's a cutie," Daisy said.

"Yes, she sure is. A total sweetheart, too, even more so than Loren," I said.

Daisy's eyebrows raised. "That's hard to imagine."

"I know, right? I mean, Loren was my first love, but Kara is something special, she loves everyone, including other dogs."

"Awesome."

"So, how are you?"

"Good. I'm evaluating dogs for the Humane Society now, which has its ups and downs."

*"Hey, where's my T-shirt?"*

Our eyes locked for a second.

I knew what that meant. Daisy had the power to decide a dog's fate, whether or not it was deemed adoptable or rescue worthy.

I knew she would wield that power in the most benevolent, responsible way, but it must be a heavy burden to carry.

People were starting to filter in and Daisy was soon swept away in a sea of hugs and handshakes. I sat alone at the signing table and ordered fries with buffalo sauce, macaroni and cheese, and a side Caesar salad.

I'd like to say that I didn't miss the wings, but truth be told, I envied the people gnawing on those bones without a care in the world.

I just kept remembering Mario the chicken as they did so and assured myself a few moments of carnivorous satisfaction wasn't worth the price.

## Buckets O' Fun

Outside the restaurant was a tall sign proclaiming "We Had Buckets O' Fun!" Above the photo of an overflowing buck of wings were two cutouts.

"I want a shot of me and Kara!" I said to the group helping us out to the car. Every once in a while, no matter how hard I tried, the geeky tourist in me just couldn't be contained.

A kind male volunteer put down my box of books, picked up Kara and held her next to me behind the cutout.

My grin was much wider than hers in the photo. Poor Kara, stuck with such a dork for an aunt.

*"Really, Aunt Michelle?"*

\*\*\*

Kara and I were set for some fun in the sun the next morning, a Sunday. It was the Western Pennsylvania Humane Society's Pup Walk taking place at a new waterfront mall. Our table was not shaded and there wasn't much traffic in our section, but we enjoyed the camaraderie. Hundreds of dogs were there, some looking for homes, the others a proud family member being shown off by their owners.

It was so hot, kiddy pools were set on the grass for dogs to dive into. I took Kara over for a dunk. She needed to be led, one stubby leg at a time, over the rim into the water. Kerplunk. Once Kara was in, she looked up at me, confused.

"Why am I here?" her eyes implored.

I splashed water on Kara's fur, which shined a brilliant gold in the sunlight. "Doesn't that feel good?" I cooed.

Apparently not. Kara hightailed it out of the pool as soon as she could.

Pit Stops 2

"Seriously?" I asked her. "I'd love to go for a swim right about now!"

Once on the grass, she shook the water off, splashing me in the process. I didn't mind at all. Kara led me back to the table, so she could get some attention from Susie Gilbert. Susie and I met on the last trip. She was once the WPHS adoption counselor, but had since left to do social work with people, her original profession.

"It was just too hard," Susie had told me. "Though working with people isn't exactly easy. I had a patient try to attack me in the parking lot recently."

"Geez, what happened?" I asked in horror.

"He was off his meds and just went berserk. Security came, but it was scary."

"I bet."

*"Thanks for the bling, Susie."*

"I'm not sure if I made the right decision sometimes, leaving," Susie said. "But I still get to volunteer with the dogs and keep up Super Seven."

Super Seven was the pit bull training program Susie originally implemented during her time at WPHS. It increased the pit adoption rate and Susie continued to help train the dogs.

Since I'm not a sports fan, Susie had to point out Charlie Batch of the Pittsburgh Steelers, the event's honored guest, to me. What the hell. I

## Buckets O' Fun

walked up with Kara and asked him to pose for a photo with us, which Charlie did graciously. It turned out he and his wife, Tasha, had a rescued pit and Rottweiler. Tasha even bought a book.

Susie, meanwhile, bought Kara a cool, custom white scarf with "KARA" airbrushed on it in hot pink graffiti lettering. I immediately put it on her. "Kara's got bling," I said proudly as Kara put her paws on Susie's legs and reached up to kiss her.

"Well, she's a star, she needs some bling," Susie said, hugging Kara tight. "Don't you?"

The sun was unrelenting at our unsheltered table. I asked our neighbor, a photographer with a canopied tent, if we could share her space. She graciously said yes and we struck up a conversation. The photographer specialized in pet portraits and donated a portion of her proceeds to WPHS.

"That's great," I said. "Do you have any dogs?"

"Yes, I have a Burmese Mountain Dog," she said. "I love those dogs. It's our second."

Uh oh. Anytime someone told me they had a purebred, a breed that they "loved" and had a history with, there was a good chance they did not rescue it.

"Oh, where did you get it?" I asked casually, dreading the answer.

The photographer looked meek for a moment. "From a breeder."

I shook my head and frowned. I am not known for my poker face.

"I know," she said. "I tried, but it's so hard to find a rescued Burmese Mountain Dog."

"I can appreciate that, but why did you have to get a purebred? You know from dealing with WPHS how many dogs die because people shop rather than adopt."

"We just really love the breed. I try to help the shelter in other ways."

"That's really nice of you to help the shelter, but the number one thing you could've done to help them is adopt a dog." The heat had put me in a mood and not a diplomatic one. "I may have wanted a certain kind of dog, but I found my last two. Both were pit bull mixes. It wasn't easy, they fought sometimes, but I made it work. Because if I didn't and turned them into a shelter, I knew they would die and I couldn't live with that."

The woman looked at me, taken aback, but I was on a roll.

"Before that, I took in my sister's two middle-aged dogs because she had her first kid and didn't have time for them anymore. Sometimes people should do what's right, rather than just doing what they want."

"I understand what you're saying, but…" she said before I cut her off.

"Do you? Because until people stop buying from breeders and pet stores, dogs at shelters are going to die. I can't just be cool with that, for whatever reason. Sorry."

She looked at me, a grimace on her face while an awkward silence formed. Really, what else was there to say?

"Thanks for the shade," I said, gathering Kara and leaving the comfort of the canopy.

The event wasn't over, but it was definitely time for us to go.

***

My fantasy was coming true. As Kara relaxed inside the air-conditioned comfort of the Courtad home, gnawing on her latest toy, I was sprawled on the wicker couch on the porch, iced tea in one hand, a book in the other. After seeing those young kids' perfect bodies, I couldn't bring myself to sport a bathing suit, but I could still get away with a tank top and shorts.

While Rebecca was in the kitchen making crab cakes, Mike was hard at work at the barbecue station, where he was clearly in his domain. Cee Lo Green belted out "Forget You" while sports played silently on a TV hanging overhead. It was a very nice set up.

"What are you making?" I asked, having wandered over to the bar to see. Besides eating, cooking is one of my favorite pastimes and I'm always looking for new ideas.

"A seafood boil, with shrimp, scallops, mussels, corn and potatoes," he said as my face lit up.

"You're kidding! That's like my favorite meal!"

"Really?"

"Truly! I eat it whenever I'm in the south and try to make it at home, too. How do you do it?"

"Just boil it up with Old Bay and serve it with drawn butter."

Buckets O' Fun

"Sounds perfect. I can't wait," I said, smiling broadly and returned to sprawl on the outdoor sofa. This was the life.

Shortly thereafter, the guests started to arrive: Geri, Carrie, Jessica, Lynn, Michele, Mary Ann and Abby (who gave Loren her first taste of frozen custard). All of them were or had been WPHS volunteers. Some brought their significant others to the party.

These men really supported their women's rescue efforts, which was something I appreciated. Wayde wasn't into fostering or going to help me clean kennels, but his willingness to take care of our dogs while I went on the road and also paying for my book to be published showed me how much he really cared.

It was heaven just enjoying a sunny afternoon with new friends, eating great food. We talked about dogs mostly, sometimes about men or the state of the world. I finally started to feel like I could unwind,

*"Did someone say fetch?"*

relax, take a breath. Rebecca was an amazing hostess, making everyone feel right at home. I know I certainly did. Leaving the next day for a soulless hotel was not appealing.

Kara was enjoying the party, too. Michele Carso, in particular, had developed a deep affection for her, both at the party and the Hello Bully event the night before, threatening to kidnap Kara to come live with her. She already had a nine-year old shelter pit rescue named Nola, whom she trained as a Canine Good Citizen and therapy dog, but I didn't doubt Michele for a second.

Michele had brought Kara a squeak toy, which she demolished in minutes, and a glow in the dark ball. Whenever I would look for Kara, inevitably, she was sitting in Michele's lap or they were off in the yard, playing a game of fetch.

"If you don't find a home for Kara, please tell her foster mom I want her," Michele said.

Rebecca told me the same thing as we departed on Monday morning. She had her hands full with Riley, as well as Tre and her other dog, but Rebecca had developed a soft spot for Kara.

"I'll drive to California for Kara if her foster will let me have her," she said, petting Kara goodbye through the car window. "I'm serious, I will."

"I believe you," I replied, looking over at Kara, grinning and ready to go in the passenger seat. "But somehow, I think Kyle is going to have a very hard time giving Kara up."

# Outlaws

Our next stop was Louisville, Kentucky, where we had nothing planned but to catch up on laundry and sleep. The most natural route to Louisville is through Ohio, which I had avoided with Loren. This time, a little tired and distracted, I didn't realize we were headed towards the state with one of the strongest breed-specific legislation stances until we crossed the border and saw the Ohio state sign.

I gulped, looking over at Kara, who, as usual, was sleeping and oblivious to the outside world. It was hard to believe that this innocent creature could be in danger just for being born a bully breed, to possibly be murdered for looking a certain way. While I knew that Denver had a history of taking pit bulls out of homes and killing them at shelters, I didn't believe that this was the case in Ohio. Especially for an out-of-state traveler and a dog that wasn't even hers.

Heart thumping in my chest, I decided to take the chance of driving the interstate straight through to Kentucky, traveling at or just a few miles above the speed limit. How long could it be, anyway?

Hours. It was hours of endless asphalt. Tried as I might to hold it, my bladder betrayed me and I had to find a restroom. My fear was being caught by a cop, so we pulled over to a rather remote, swampy little gas station. I parked in the back and said a quick prayer, hitting my lock key twice before I ventured inside.

Kara was up in her seat when I returned. She, too, had to make a potty break.

"OK, girl, but make it quick," I said, looking left and right before letting her out of the car. Kara was now able to jump out of the car, albeit in a funny way, hurling her stumpy body fearlessly to the ground. She landed onto the hot pavement, then we headed to some tall weeds so Kara could do her business.

I keep glancing and turning to make sure we weren't being watched. "Hurry," I told her. Seriously, I felt like some kind of criminal, like the lookout or getaway driver on a robbery. It was not a good feeling, something my law-abiding, sober self wasn't used to.

Kara took her sweet time, happily snuffling yards of ground before she finally squatted and tinkled. Relieved, I cut her sniffing short and led Kara back to the car, lifting her quickly into the passenger seat and rushing back to my side of the car.

Kara, who had barely settled in, jerked back when I peeled out of the parking lot and sped up the highway onramp.

"I think we did it, Kare Bear," I told her. "Just keep it on the DL, OK?"

She looked back at me with tranquil golden eyes, before sighing and settling her big head onto the front of the seat. Kara wasn't bothered, but I was still freaked out that we might get caught. If it wasn't so hot, I would've covered her up with that fuzzy pink blanket.

No matter how bad I had to go, that would be the one and only pee break in Ohio for us. I wasn't willing to chance it twice. Thankfully, a billboard pronouncing "Welcome to Kentucky" appeared on the horizon before my bladder gave way. I was never so happy to see a state sign in my life.

Louisville was home to the Kentucky Derby, which I found out when we drove by the vacant convention center and race track. The town itself seemed empty and somewhat downtrodden, at least on the stretch of road where our hotel was located. It wasn't lush and green, as I'd hoped. It was straight city, with a smattering of suburb on the side. Oh, well. I just wanted to rest, anyway, and Kara was cool wherever we went.

The hotel did have one advantage. In the back was a huge, full lawn and no one around using it.

"You know what time it is, Kara?" I said, pulling a small, newly acquired Kong out of my pocket. She knew alright. As soon as Kara saw that flash of red, she got into position, her stout body taut, her eyes fixated on my hand. I hurled the toy as far as I could and watched the little low-rider turn into a world-class athlete. Kara dove for the Kong, rolling three times, before popping up with it in her mouth. I would cheer whenever she hurled herself into the air and caught it before hitting the ground. This was about one in every 10 to 15 throws.

Panting after about 10 minutes, she dropped the slobbery Kong at my feet. There was a dog barking behind the concrete wall, though I couldn't see it. I felt bad that Kara was having so much fun and the unseen canine wasn't.

Soon, we had visitors. A young couple - he tall and lanky in skinny jeans, she voluptuous with oversized sunglasses and shaggy hair – walked up to the grass. At the end of a leash the woman was holding was an incredibly tiny terrier mix that probably weighed about three pounds.

"She's friendly," I called out, wondering if they thought Kara would eat their little dog.

"Is she?" The girl said, immediately rushing over to meet Kara. "I'm so glad. I love pit bulls!"

Kara obliged as she bent down, standing up on her compact legs and reaching for a kiss.

"Oh, you are such a sweetheart!" the young woman said, hugging Kara, her own dog briefly forgotten. "I love you!"

"And who's this?" I asked, nodding toward her dog.

"This is Betsy. She's a rescue. I'm a volunteer at a shelter in Cincinnati. I'm Erica and this is Adam."

We all shook hands.

"So, you're in Ohio? Aren't they really harsh with pit bulls?" I asked. "I was afraid to drive across the state with Kara, fearing a cop would pull us over and take her to a shelter."

"Well, they won't just take a dog from someone and kill it, like Denver."

I took a deep breath. "Whew. That's a relief."

"I mean, it's still not great for pit bulls. It's hard to get them out of the shelter. So, where did you get Kara?"

"Well, actually Kara's not my dog," I said and launched into our story, still throwing the ball for Kara. Erica, Adam and Betsy were a welcome addition to the Louisville landscape. Maybe this would be a fun stay after all.

"That's really cool," Erica said. "Like I said, I love pits. There's one at the shelter right now that I'm really working hard on to find a home." She whipped out her phone and showed me his picture.

Funny world we live in. No one pulls out a wallet full of photos anymore. It was kind of Star Trek, really, if you were born before 1985, which I suspected Erica was not.

"Oh, I wish you the best of luck. He's really cute," I said. "So, what brings you two down here?"

"We're going to a concert," Adam said. "But we're trying to figure out what to do with Betsy."

I didn't hesitate. "I'll watch her."

"Really?" Erica asked. "That would be awesome! I'm warning you, though, Betsy's a real mama's girl. She might cry for me."

"No worries. We'll make it work."

Watching a strange dog was not something I'd usually offer up, but I intuitively trusted Erica and Adam would come back for Betsy. If not, Betsy wouldn't take up much room and I could probably find a home or rescue for her by the time we made it back to California. Kara seemed to like her fine, though Betsy seemed a little overwhelmed by Kara's size and curiosity.

We exchanged cell phone numbers and Erica, all dressed up, delivered Betsy to our door at 7 p.m.

"Have fun!" I said, slightly envious. I hardly ever went to concerts anymore. The older I got, the less I wanted to deal with crowds and parking, not to mention staying up late.

As Erica and Adam enjoyed their night, Kara, Betsy and I watched TV. Well, Kara and I did anyway. Betsy was either crying, running to the door, or jumping on and off the bed for the first few hours. She finally mellowed out, falling asleep in a big leather chair by the TV, but immediately woke up when her mama came to pick her up around midnight, crying at the door before returning to Erica's arms.

"We'd love to return the favor and watch Kara tomorrow morning, if you want to run errands or anything," Erica told me.

"Are you sure?" I asked, slightly groggy. Besides never going to concerts, I rarely stayed up past 10 p.m., so this late evening exchange was unusual.

"Oh my God, I would love to watch her!" Erica told me. "I want to snuggle with her!'"

The next morning, I dropped Kara off to a bleary-eyed Erica and attended a long overdue A.A. meeting, then headed to Mirage Mediterranean Food across the street. If you're trying to stick to a vegetarian diet, Mediterranean food makes it pretty easy. I had a savory, aromatic vegetable stir fry over fluffy brown rice, topped off with a flaky, sweet piece of baklava and a few gallons of iced tea, consumed while reading the local paper. I missed Kare Bear, but it was nice to have a few moments to myself, too.

A text came from Kyle. "Asking Jim if we can keep Kara." Jim was Kyle's husband and while remarkably patient over the last decade that the Harris' had fostered and adopted shelter dogs, it was my understanding he was tiring of the process since his recent retirement from teaching.

I called Kyle. "You must really miss Kara, huh?"

"I do. She's so special. It took her being away to realize I can't live without her."

"Do you think Jim will let you have another dog? I thought he was kind of over it?"

Kyle sighed. "Well, I told him that I would stop fostering if we could keep Kara."

"You? Stop fostering? Ha! I mean, that's great news for Kara…"

"Well, I'm getting old and my back hurts. It's hard for me to do all the poop scooping and bending. I figured I could work on making Kara a therapy dog and do education instead."

"Well, she'd be perfect for it, but you know that."

It was now noon, my designated time to pick up Kara. Erica, who arranged for a late checkout, was reluctant to let her go.

"She's the best. She just laid down and snuggled with us. I'm gonna miss you, Kara." Erica leaned down for one last smooch and beamed when she got it. I got a hug, too.

We hadn't gone for our morning walk yet, so I took Kara out to explore the neighborhood. On the corner, down from the hotel, was a small, grungy bar that looked as if it held a wild party the night before. Down the street were some modest homes, so we headed that way.

The mystery barking dog from the day before revealed itself about six houses in. It was a big German Shepherd stuck in a small pen. There were no cars in the driveway, so I tentatively took Kara up closer to investigate.

The floor was dried mud, there was about an inch of mucky water in a rusty metal bowl and the fluffy dog looked extremely uncomfortable on a hot, humid summer's day. Thankfully, the pen was under a tree for shade, but that was about the only amenity.

"You poor thing," I told the dog, who wagged his tail furiously as we approached, no longer barking. He seemed friendly, but I wasn't about to take a chance sticking my fingers into his cage.

I was pissed. If this was indeed the same dog we had heard off and on the day before, I suspected he was in that pen for hours on end, maybe even permanently. This broke my heart.

Back at the hotel, I posted the situation on Facebook, asking for advice on what I should do. Some people said call animal control, the more radical ones said steal the dog. Besides the fact that his pen was secured with a locked chain, what would I do with him then? Take the dog to a shelter? What outcome would that bring? There was no way I could fit him in the car with me and Kara. It was overloaded with our travel gear, plus how would he react? My first concern had to be Kara and not getting arrested for stealing someone's property…which dogs are, according to the law. Spending time in a Southern jail was not on our agenda.

What I did do was email the local humane society to let them know about the situation, as well as call animal control with the dog's address. Animal control told me that as long as the dog had shelter and water, that there was nothing illegal about its conditions. (I also found out, by doing a little research, that owning a pit bull within Cincinnati city limits was illegal and had been since 2003. How very sad and how very glad I was that we did not stop there).

Still not satisfied about the German Shepherd situation, I wrote a note to the owner:

*Hello,*

*I'm traveling through the area and noticed your dog was in a pen with very little water on an extremely hot day. It is not healthy for your dog to be kept in such conditions. If you cannot make your dog a member of your family and bring him inside your home, or create a larger yard for him, I hope you do the right thing and find someone else to adopt your dog or take it to your local no-kill shelter.*

*Thank you,*

*A concerned dog lover*

We hoped in the car to deliver the message. There was no sign of life at the house and the German Shepherd was still in his pen. I folded the note and placed it behind the metal detail on the screen door, somewhere noticeable. Then I walked over to the pen and gave Nylabone to the grateful dog. He sniffed it and a few seconds later, licked my hand through a metal slit.

"I hope this helps," I told him, tears welling in my eyes. "I hope you get a better life."

My journalistic nature couldn't leave it at that, however. I had to find out more information. I left Kara in the car with the A/C running and knocked on a door a few houses down. Through the glass front door, I could see many unpacked moving boxes. A heavyset woman walked out from the hall, looked at me curiously and opened the door a crack.

"Sorry to bother you, but do you know anything about the German Shepherd living a few houses down from you?"

"No, actually, we just moved here."

"OK, thanks."

I went to the next house. A brassy blonde senior with a raspy voice opened the door about halfway, eyeing me suspiciously.

"Hi, sorry to bother you. Do you know anything about the German Shepherd living next door?"

"Yes, why?"

"Well, I noticed that he lives in a very small pen with little water and it's really hot out. That's not a good environment for any dog," I said. "Is he kept like that all the time?"

"I don't think so. His owner really seems to love him. He takes the dog for walks and from what I see, treats him fine, like it's his best friend."

"Alright. Thank you."

"You're welcome," the woman said, closing the door as quickly as she could. She probably didn't get accosted by crazy dog ladies every day.

Her information made me feel a bit better. Perhaps this was just a case of the owner being gone and needing to keep his dog in a pen for longer than usual.

The next day, a text from Kyle arrived as we were waking up. "Keeping Kara" it said. I texted back a happy face.

Kara was snoring away, her body outstretched, her massive head deeply nestled into a snow-white pillow. She was a great sleeper and looked completely adorable doing it, like a furry little manatee, so peaceful and serene.

I snuggled up next to Kara and kissed the top of her head. "Guess what, Pookie La La?" The nickname had just started the week before, but Kara was already starting to respond to it. "You've got a home. Auntie Kyle is now Mama Kyle."

She cracked open her eyes, peered at me sleepily, then licked my face. I rubbed her belly and started to cry tears of joy. Kara had a true family, the best mom in the whole world to return to in California. My tears fell on Kara's soft fur as we snuggled. Reluctantly, I let her go to pack up our stuff. We had miles to drive.

"Suck it up, Sathe," I said to the reflection in the hotel mirror. My eyes were red and my nose runny. "Stop being such a pussy."

As Kara and I departed Louisville, I stopped by the German Shepherd's house again. There was a car in the driveway and the dog was not in his pen. Did my letter make a difference? Was there even a problem to begin with?

That answer wasn't clear, but I hoped for the best.

# Mending Hearts and Helping Pits

A few days before departing for the book tour, there was a surprise waiting for me at the post office. It was from Nina Gaither, whom I met in Indianapolis with Loren. Curious and excited, I ripped open the plastic bubble envelope. Inside was a custom necklace Nina had made, a stamped copper pit bull profile with a little tag. Looking closely, I noticed it said "L" on one side and "K" on the other. I burst into tears. How thoughtful. How lovely.

It came at just the right time, as I was feeling anxious about setting off with Kara, about signing my new book and the sadness I would find once more across the country. The morning we left, I had put the necklace on the "K" side and wore it like a talisman just about every day since. It gave me strength when I was feeling down.

I recounted this story to Nina as we enjoyed lunch at TJ's Kitchen, a modest diner in Indianapolis, not far from her home in the suburbs. I was enjoying a perfectly deep-fried fish sandwich, the crispy crust contrasting nicely with the soft, warm bun and rich, tangy tartar sauce.

"I'm so glad you like it," Nina said. With her long blonde hair, freckled face, and bright white smile, Nina looked like a mild-mannered Midwestern girl, but she was a fierce rescue warrior. Especially for pit bulls. One of the original members of Indy Pit Crew, Nina was also a behavioral assessor for the Indianapolis Humane Society for many years.

When she worked for Indy Humane, Nina regularly attended animal control meetings. In 2008, a well-known no-kill advocate was hired as the Indianapolis Animal Care and Control Administrator. During his rambling introductory speech, the administrator failed to mention how he planned on dealing with the city's anti-adoption policy for pit bulls.

Nina stood up and asked, "Since ACC doesn't adopt out pit bulls to the public, how are they going to be handled?"

"Like any other breed," the man replied.

"My instinct was that he had planned to just adopt them out against policy. As on board with that as I would have been, I was asking in the public forum hoping the official policy would be changed," Nina told me.

After the meeting, Nina walked over to introduce herself. As Nina told the man she was looking forward to working with him, he gave her what is commonly referred to as stink eye and said, "I really wanted to tell you to shut up."

That attitude only fueled her fire. As a member of Indy Pit Crew, an advocacy group and foster network that also provides low-cost spay or neuter, training, food and other resources to pit bull owners, Nina began to legally move pit bulls out of the county shelter in the summer of 2009. She performed temperament tests to select the most adoptable pits and the shelter cooperated by allocating six or seven kennels to house the dogs.

Once fosters or adopters were found, the dogs were pulled through rescued and placed in homes; 42 pit bulls were saved this way.

Now an events administrator for Indiana War Memorial, Nina continues temperament testing dogs for Indy Pit Crew and Mended Hearts Indy. Nina's dog, Lex, was the first International Police Working Dog Association-certified cadaver pit bull. Lex passed away in 2010.

The Gaither pack currently included Coal, a gorgeous grey pit bull; Gilly, a sweet, silly young pit/Border collie; and two Dachshunds, Way Low Way Long and Oscar, who, in typical little dog fashion, rule the roost.

Nina and her husband Adam kindly hosted us at their home for this trip. Kara was in heaven as soon as she saw the dozens of Kongs, Nylabones and real bones for her to choose from. They were spread all over the hardwood floor and rugs in the living room.

It was almost sensory overload for Kara. She went from one toy to another to another, until she finally settled on a familiar Kong. Nina watched with loving amusement.

"Help yourself, Kara," she said.

We went outside to the backyard. Fetch took on a different tone, both of us avoiding the in-ground pool so Kara wouldn't drown.

Once Kara was a little worn out, Nina put Coal on a leash and we all went for a walk.

Mending Hearts and Helping Pits

The two were semi-interested in one another, sniffing all the right body parts, but not overtly engaged.

"This is good," Nina told me. I was a nervous auntie and she knew it. The last thing I wanted was for Kara to get injured. "This is just the right amount of attention."

"Good," I said, trying to relax, knowing my tension made its way down the leash to Kara. She was trotting along happily next to Coal now.

Once we reconvened in the backyard and the dogs were off leash,

*"However do I choose, Aunt Nina?"*

they were free to really get to know one another. They were flirting, Coal prancing about, Kara jumping back and wiggling her booty.

"Looks like a summer romance is brewing," Nina said as I laughed.

A few minutes later, the infatuation was coming to an end. There was a minor scuffle over a toy and the two snapped at one another fairly forcefully, which freaked me out.

Nina and I ran over to break it up.

"Alright, play time is over," I scolded the dogs.

"They should be fine, Michelle. They're just working it out," Nina tried to reassure me.

Pit Stops 2

*"Hey Kara, check out my moves!"*

"Nina, I know I'm being a spaz, but can we separate them for a while? I just can't risk something happening to Kara."

Being the gracious hostess that she was, Nina put Coal back in his crate. During our stay, we rotated the dogs out separately. Nina's pack had the run of the house when Kara and I were out or asleep and vice versa. The sisterly companionship with Nina and the warmth of being in a home rather than a hotel was very welcoming.

Every morning, I awoke to Nina hammering out jewelry in her little studio in the downstairs foyer. Generous Nina donated a portion of each sale to a rescue organization and oftentimes just donated the necklaces outright for rescues to raise money. I touched my Kara/Loren necklace and smiled.

\*\*\*

We had a hectic schedule in Indianapolis, with four signings in three days. The first was at Three Dog Bakery in the Broad Ripple section of town for Mended Hearts Indy. Nichole Heilbron, who founded the organization with Nina, immediately grasped me into a bear hug upon meeting. Nichole had kind brown eyes, upbeat energy and a quick wit. Our conversation was easy from the start. She was a San Diego native, so perhaps it was the California connection that bonded us quickly. That and our mutual love for animals.

Nichole, an IT consultant, and her husband Aaron moved to Indianapolis a few years prior for work. Proud parents of a rescued, injured pit bull whom they acquired in California, Nichole and Aaron first hooked into the area's rescue community as volunteers for Indy Pit Crew, which is how they met Nina.

Mended Hearts Indy and Indy Pit Crew share many of the same volunteers. Emily and Matt Loman, a young couple with two pit bulls, and Kerry Anderson and Miranda Paige, permanent and foster pit parents, were some of the rising stars.

Miranda brought a sweet young foster pit mix named Fawn to the signing. A couple in their 20s had come by to meet Fawn and potentially adopt her. It was quite a scene in the hip, crowded dog-themed bakery, between volunteers and supporters, people getting books signed, Fawn and her entourage, Kara and hers, everyone cooing and hugging and kissing dogs that many in mainstream society looked upon as vicious predators. If only everyone could see what we saw.

Following the book signing, Nichole and I were walking along with Kara when we were stopped by a man driving a Mercedes with a handsome blue pit bull riding shotgun.

"Is that a pit bull?" he asked, smiling down at Kara. "Beautiful dog."

"Yes," I replied. "You have a good-looking dog, too."

"Are you going to get him fixed?" Nichole asked, starting to fish an Indy Pit Crew card out of her purse.

"Noooo," the man said slowly, "I'm not going to fix him."

At the same time, a young blonde woman overheard our conversation and ran towards the car with her iPhone.

"My brother breeds pit bull puppies. Wanna see?" she showed the man.

Nichole and I looked at each other in disbelief.

"Did you know 3,000 pit bulls were killed in Indianapolis shelters last year?" Nichole asked loudly.

The girl glanced up for a second. "Yeah, that's sad," she said and continued showing off her brother's new puppies. "Aren't they cute?"

We shook our heads. "You could stop breeding!" Nichole screamed as we walked away.

The girl started to answer, but I just held up a hand. "Whatever," I muttered, the hairs on my head beginning to tingle and stand on end. "Assholes."

"It makes me crazy," Nichole said. "There's dozens or hundreds of more dogs in the system from their ignorance, messes we'll have to clean up."

Nichole and I retold the story to Aaron, Nina, Matt, Emily and Miranda, who had assembled at Monon Food Company, an earthy restaurant with delicious, locally-sourced food and a patio for Kara.

"Assholes," everyone agreed.

Kara lay at my feet, assuming the platypus, worn out from her appearance and the humid summer weather. Besides the company, I enjoyed a Greek salad and a side of macaroni and cheese with caramelized onions and Portobello mushrooms, which the restaurant was rightly famous for. After dinner, several of us capped off dinner with ice cream at BRICS, a local institution a few blocks down, where I ravished a large scoop of cookies and cream with piping hot fudge. Kara had a little dish of plain vanilla. I'm not sure who enjoyed it more. City life definitely had its advantages.

***

Though packed, our scheduled allowed us time for a little fun. For Kara, that meant a spa day with Brandy Bennett of All Creatures Great and Groomed, whom I had met on Facebook.

We had driven through many different landscapes of Indianapolis to get there. Nina and Adam lived in a very suburban, park-like setting. Other parts of the city were grittier, working-class, with an industrial feel. Outside one dilapidated home with broken shingles and windows, there was a young couple in stained old clothes, smoking cigarettes and watching two toddlers run around in the dirt, wearing only droopy diapers. It was hot and humid outside. I could practically smell the sweat and smoke from my car.

Some neighborhoods looked rather affluent, with brand new brick and plantation-style apartment buildings and schools. Just a little down the road, large groups of people congregated on stoops, around old cars or on bicycles. Seemingly capable adults shooting the breeze at the time of day when most other people were at work led me to believe that this wasn't gentrification but poverty, pure and simple.

At the groomers, Kara was welcomed with open arms, which she trotted right into. Brandy hugged and kissed Kara before Erin, the

## Mending Hearts and Helping Pits

salon owner's tween daughter, took over, leading Kara back into the grooming area, where she went with nary a glance backward at me.

"Should I paint her nails?" Brandy asked me excitedly.

This was new. "Do people do that with their dogs?"

"Yeah, it's really cute. Especially on a dog like Kara."

"Why not? We're on vacation…well at least, she is. Go for it!"

"What color?"

"Surprise me."

While Kara was being pampered, I had a date a few miles across town with Nichole to learn more about Mended Hearts Indy.

In September 2010, Nichole and Nina took in a three month old orange and white pit bull puppy with tapeworm from a high-kill Indianapolis shelter. They named her Loren (in you-know-who's honor, which thrilled me) and nursed the puppy back to health at a foster home. Today, Loren, renamed Teddy Bear, is healthy, happy and loving life with her forever family.

"I have a soft spot for the neglected, the abandoned, the abused," Nichole told me over lunch at Acropolis, an old-school Greek restaurant in Indianapolis with terrific taramasalata and so-so spanakopita. "I realized it's not just a pit bull thing for me, it's a broken dog thing."

Loren was the first official rescue for Mended Hearts Indy, which focuses on sick or injured dogs that are usually the first in line for euthanizing at shelters. The organization's first unofficial rescue, before they received non-profit status, was a blind black lab mix named Ray, who was languishing away in a Gary, Indiana shelter with a softball-sized growth on his neck.

"Something about his photo struck me. I just couldn't let that dog die," she said.

Nichole posted a ChipIn, an online fundraising application, to her Facebook page and raised Ray's estimated $1,500 vet bill to remove the blocked salivary gland.

"People are so generous, they really want to help these dogs," Nichole said. "We get what we need and sometimes more, which allows us to help other dogs."

Since then, Mended Hearts alumni have grown to include Sachi, a surrendered pit bull who was so emaciated her vertebrae and ribs stood out like a relief map (cruelty charges against the owner were pending), and Roxie, a huge Rottweiler mix who was going to be euthanized due to lack of space at a shelter. Both were still in foster homes.

"These dogs are rock stars," Nichole said proudly. "I just don't know why they haven't been adopted yet."

Mended Hearts hosts adoption events throughout the city at least three times a week, at restaurants and bars that line the trendier neighborhoods. Several dogs have found homes that way.

Occasionally, Mended Hearts will rescue a terminal dog. "Even if it's just for a week, they're in a home, being loved and cared for," Nichole said, her warm brown eyes turning glossy. "It's the least we can do, to show them a little kindness. It's better than dying in a shelter, scared and alone."

***

*"I'm too sexy for my paws…"*

Kara was sporting bright red nails, which attracted attention as we navigated the crowded streets downtown for a potty break. Was it my imagination or did the manicure add a little more strut to her step?

"Wow, look at that dog," a passerby said.

"Did you see her nails?" said another to her friend. "How adorable!"

Some people even whistled or called out to Kara as

they drove by. "Hey pretty dog!"

Kyle was not amused by her dog's makeover, which I had posted a picture of on Facebook.

"OMG. She looks totally embarrassed!" Kyle wrote.

"Kyle, don't be mad at me. LOL. She looks a bit tarty...but everyone loved it! It's almost worn off today," I wrote back.

Like with human nieces and nephews, aunties could get away with a lot, especially when they were thousands of miles from home.

Our signing at the downtown branch of Three Dog Bakery had been pretty quiet. Afterwards me, Kara, Aaron, Nichole and Nina, made our way to dinner at Yats, a grungy brownstone bar with a variety of etouffees served up to hungry college kids. I had the crawfish and vegetarian options, served over a mound of white rice and accompanied by a thick slab of crispy, buttery garlic bread for $7. While not up to the etouffees I've had in New Orleans, the stew was hearty, comforting and tasty, especially for the price.

It was a Friday night, everyone was pretty mellow from a long week, except for Aaron, Nichole's husband, who was holding court, telling funny tales as the rest of us dug into our food and Kara snoozed by my feet. He belonged to a comedic improvisational group and his witty observations, delivered with a frantic energy, had us all busting up. I loved the Indy peeps, their sense of community, their laughter, their camaraderie. Should I find myself in need of a cross-country move someday, Indianapolis, along with Pittsburgh, was pretty high up on the list.

"How would you like a private tour of the War Memorial?" Nina asked me as we walked back to our cars. "It's really pretty spectacular, especially when you get it all to yourself. Tomorrow will be crazy, so it's best if we do it now."

Nina was talking about the InPride Festival, a popular gay pride event being held at the war memorial. Indy Pit Crew had a booth and I was scheduled to do an appearance after a signing at Indy Humane.

"Let's go," I said. Kara was content to sleep in the car, with the windows cracked open to let in some of the night air, while Nina proudly showed me where she went to work each day. It was incredible, with three floors, miles of green and white marble, brass accents and imposing statues of famous war figures.

She gave me a history of each section. Nina, who had served in the Navy, was clearly patriotic, while I struggled with my feelings about military and war. Since World War II, my sense was that there had not been a good reason for grown men, and now women, to kill each other. At least not for the noble auspices given by politicians or the rich and powerful as they lined their own pockets, garnered influence or oppressed other cultures. I hated the game, not the players, so I fully supported veterans and have even been known to donate a few bucks to their cause when I could. War is just something I'll never understand. There has to be a better way.

Like Oz behind the curtain, Nina led me through the belly of the building, to an old elevator with metal doors she had to manually open and shut, then through a long, dark hallway to a theater with hundreds of ornate, red velvet chairs.

"Go stand on the stage," Nina said, flicking some levers until a spotlight shone on the mahogany floors. I walked over to the podium and looked upon the cavernous emptiness. So this was what it was like to be important, I thought.

"Remember, don't shop, adopt! Spay and neuter your pets...oh, and pit bulls are great dogs," I intoned to the non-existent audience as Nina silently applauded behind me.

\*\*\*

InPride attracted 30,000 attendees, some subtle, most flamboyant. There were obese men and women decked out in the tiniest bikinis to young club kids painted with rainbows to gorgeous drag queens decked out in the latest fashions.

"Did you ever notice that all drag queens are tall?" Nina asked me as we scooted through the crowds in her War Memorial golf cart. It was like the parting of the rainbow sea.

"So true," I said.

"There has to be a connection..."

"Well, maybe if someone's that tall, they have to become basketball players or drag queens. Or if you're Dennis Rodman, you do both."

Nina guffawed. "That's it, that's the connection!"

The Indy Pit Crew booth was a hit with guests, largely due to the pit bull kissing booth. Kissers included Mended Heart fosters Fawn and Harper, a brindle beauty healing from a leg injury. Though advertised as free, kiss recipients generously donated $1 to $20 per smooch.

With the upbeat music and colorful people, the mood inside the Indy Pit Crew booth was festive. I watched with pride and happiness as Matt, Emily, Miranda and Carissa Buis Abney reached out to the community, pitching the plight of the pit bull with ease and authority, enticing more than a few to sign up for more information or to volunteer.

"It means something to be in Indy Pit Crew and our volunteers are so passionate. I'll see them post on Facebook that they got to educate someone that day and how good it made them feel," Nina said with pride. "It's so cool."

It was cool. I sat in the corner, next to my books, entertained by the scene around me. Volunteer Carissa Buis Abney was holding her dog up like a child and kissing her. Nichole and Miranda were manning the kissing booth and cheering the dogs on as they performed their task with aplomb.

*"It's a rough job, but someone's gotta do it..."*

Aaron, who could be cast as the younger, better-looking brother of Quentin Tarantino, was particularly popular at this event. He relayed a story of being offered $100 to show his, well, you can imagine to the volunteers in the booth. "I told the guy that I stopped doing that after I got married," Aaron quipped.

Matt, who was very stocky, knotted his grey Indy Pit Crew t-shirt to emulate some of the more colorful attendees, making us all laugh, while Josh did a little go-go dance with his pit bull by his side.

"You gotta stay positive," Matt said. "We see and hear all these sad stories, but you gotta stay positive."

The day ended with an impromptu pool and pizza party at Nina's house. It was wonderful to float in the pool, my arms tucked around a foam tube, my legs drifting as aimlessly as my thoughts.

Emily was doing the same next to me.

"Are you having fun?" she asked.

"Yes, this is great. You guys have been so incredible to me and Kara. You're all so wonderful. I really admire what you're doing."

Emily looked at me for a second. "Well, you're the celebrity here."

I laughed bitterly. "Yeah, right. Some celebrity. World-famous author."

"You should just own it," Emily said seriously.

Startled, I smiled nervously. "Thanks, Emily. That's really cool."

Not sure what to do next, I dove underwater, and then exited the pool. Celebrity. Ha. If only. Then maybe I would meet my goal. I was nowhere near it. Nor was I getting the national publicity I'd hope, which I felt would really help these dogs.

It seemed I would go home a failure, at least in my eyes. The thought brought stinging tears. Refocus, I told myself, settling on the grass and observing the scene around me.

Kara was the real star of the show as Aaron and Adam hoisted her onto a floating mesh mattress contraption.

She looked concerned, her ears at Defcon 5, but Kara also loved the attention of being petted and encouraged along her watery travels.

A few minutes were enough for Kara, so Adam and Aaron helped her to the pool steps.

She saw me and walked over, shaking off the wetness and relishing the solid ground beneath her feet. I hugged Kara close to my side and looked up at the sky, which was turning from sunflower to midnight blue.

Around me, everyone was laughing, drinking and enjoying a Saturday night with friends. Nichole, who was studying for a college test, came later. She rolled up her capris and stuck her legs in the water. Aaron swam over and kissed both of her kneecaps, a tender gesture that made me long for Wayde. I missed my home, my friends, my dogs, even Wayde's prissy cat Sugar Butt.

*"Hold on tight, boys!"*

Still, it was hard to be lonely in this crowd, unless I wanted to be. I got up and made my way over to the table for pizza and conversation, Kara following faithfully by my side.

# My Kind of Town

One of the fiercest animal advocates Kara and I met doesn't even own a pet. Instead, she endeavors to create a better environment for the pets and people of Chicago, including the dogs that often fall through the cracks of the judicial system.

*"Pleasure to meet you, Cynthia!"*

Cynthia Bathurst is the executive director of Safe Humane Chicago, a non-profit organization dedicated to reducing violence by showing people how kindness and compassion towards animals makes our communities safer and more humane.

Kara and I left the comfort of suburban Barrington, where we had stayed the night, to the gritty streets of Chicago to meet with Cynthia and two Safe Humane student ambassadors, Anisha Bhat and Ally Almore. Our destination was a metro police department building, a sterile place with gleaming linoleum floors and minimal ambience. The clerks gazed at me and the stubby pit bull by my side with some interest. Cynthia, who was waiting in a conference room next door, came around to give clearance and ushered us in with a wave.

Once in, Cynthia gave me a big hug, then dropped to her knees and enveloped Kara in a long, warm embrace, which Kara returned fervently, adding some kisses, too.

"Oh, aren't you just the sweetest thing?" Cynthia said, smiling at her new friend. "You are just beautiful."

Kara's little nub wagged fervently in response.

"I could just eat you up," Cynthia said with a soft Southern drawl. She's originally from Alabama, where as a kid, Cynthia grew up with dogs, cats and horses before leaving for college. Now a busy, traveling, full-time activist, pets are not in the cards for Cynthia.

"I just don't have the time, I'm too busy and never home," she explained. "Then again, I tell people, 'What do you mean, I don't have a pet?' There are 154 dogs in our court case program alone. I have so many pets. It just happens that they don't live with me.'"

In 2000, as a volunteer with Dog Advisory Work Group, Cynthia started appointing volunteer advocates for dogs at courtrooms across the city, as well as creating alliances with other community agencies. Established as Safe Humane Chicago in 2007, the organization continued attracting partners, such as local police departments, child welfare groups, and churches, to spread the message of compassion.

An effective example is Kids, Animals and Kindness, which mentors teens into becoming educators to younger children at schools across the city. "It's a very popular program. High school students want to get involved and send a message," Cynthia said. "These kids take the message out and change attitudes throughout the community. Over time, it becomes part of the cultural development."

I had seen Cynthia speak at a Best Friends No More Homeless Pets conference about three years ago. At that time, I had my hands full with The Brittany Foundation, cleaning kennels and walking dogs, trying to enlist more volunteers and creating fundraising events that would help us keep our doors open. Every fall, I was thrust into action for the annual Bow-Wows & Meows Pet Fair, a non-profit organization of which I'm a board member. We invite six L.A. county shelters to participate and in five hours on that wonderful October day, adopt out between 150-175 homeless dogs and cats.

The subjects of dog fighting, backyard breeding, animal abuse and neglect and how they connected to humanity at large were not on my radar just yet, at least not in the nuanced fashion that Cynthia had presented. Now I get it. Cynthia made animal welfare a social rather than a fringe issue. No matter how passionate and committed, a small core group of rescuers and advocates simply couldn't keep up with the demands. The animal welfare circle needed to expand dramatically, to every corner of every community, in order to affect fundamental change.

Anisha and Ally are already making a big difference at a young age. After hugging and kissing on Kara for a few minutes, they began excitedly telling me about their participation with Kids, Animals and Kindness. Anisha and Ally speak to children in grades three through six to impart the importance of proper pet ownership, how to approach

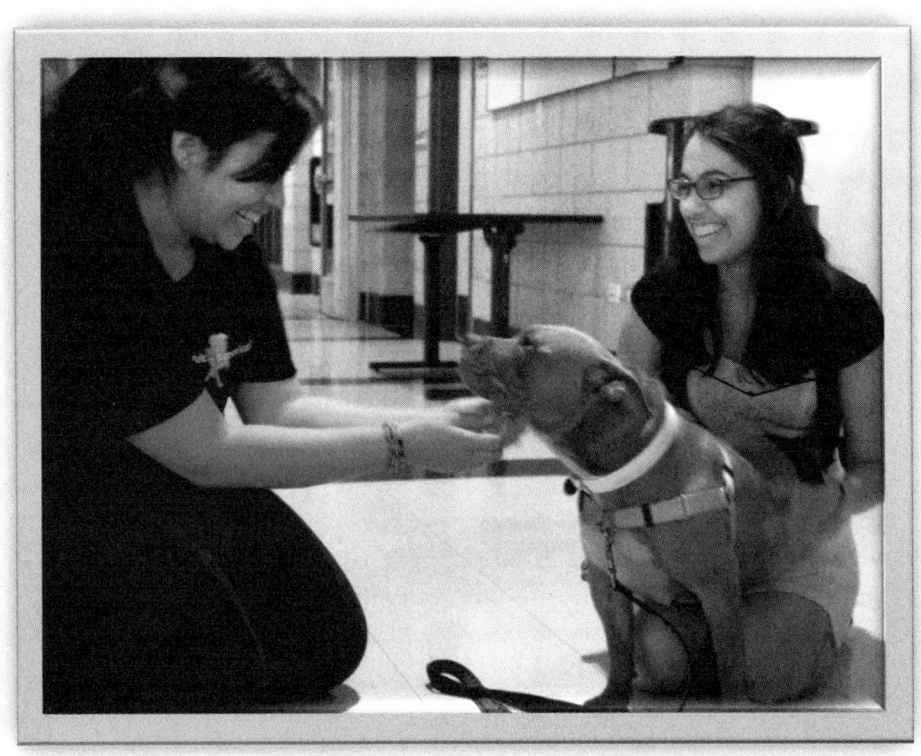

*"You help dogs like me? That's so cool!"*

stray or strange dogs and what to do when confronted with dog fighting, abuse or neglect.

"When I found out the connection in our communities with domestic violence and animal abuse, it just made sense to me," Anisha, a high school senior, said. "We talk a lot about pit bulls in our presentations, that people are often terrified of pit bulls for no reason whatsoever."

"I've loved it from day one," Ally, a high school junior, said. "There's a lot of violence towards animals in Chicago. I've even talked to my neighbors and tell them not to leave their dogs in the backyard on cold days."

Cynthia, who now practically had Kara sitting on her lap, watched the girls with obvious pride. "How do you get everyone concerned about these issues? You start with the kids," Cynthia said. "Kids relate to our youth leaders and look up to them, much more than yet another middle-aged woman telling them to do something."

In addition to its educational component, Safe Humane Chicago provides training and assessment technique for officers dealing with drug busts and other situations where dogs can become caught in the crossfire, often paying the ultimate price: with their lives.

Sergeant Cindy Schuman, a formidable woman who oversaw the officer training with Safe Humane, turned to mush when she saw Kara. She sat down and Kara scurried over for an introduction, immediately hugging Cindy's legs in a tight vise grip. Cindy looked Kara straight in the eyes, smooshed her cheeks, and accepted the first of many kisses. It was nice to know a true dog lover was the guardian of such a program and realized its full significance.

"It's a huge part of the day to day job for officers, coming into contact with dogs. Whether they're pit bulls or not, it's comforting for them to know what to look for and to have the tools in our toolbox so everyone can remain safe," Cindy said.

Safe Humane Chicago also offers programs like Lifetime Bonds at local juvenile detention centers, pairing inmates with shelter dogs for training, and Court Case Dogs, which advocates for evidence dogs left to languish at shelters after their owners are arrested.

In 2010, Dolly, a beautiful fawn pit bull who looked a lot like Kara, became the first beneficiary of the Court Case Dogs program. She had been surrendered with a litter of puppies to a municipal Chicago shelter after a domestic violence arrest that put her owner in jail. Dolly, a resource-guarder who didn't like other dogs much, was taken in by Chicago Canine Rescue Foundation for training. Eventually, a foster home was found for Dolly, who had earned her Canine Good Citizen certificate after a stint in Lifetime Bonds.

By that time, Dolly was charming and well-behaved, with a tail that wagged non-stop. She had also developed the endearing trick of lying flat on her back, all four paws in the air, begging for a belly rub. Dolly's foster father couldn't bear to let her go; she was officially adopted in 2010 by Tim Davoren.

"She wiggled and snuggled her way right into Tim's heart," Cynthia said. "Tim told me that Dolly is the queen of his condo and sleeps on his bed or the couch, when she's not being showcased at trainings or events. What could be a better outcome for a dog that's been through so much?"

Bruno was a dog that came out of a terrible abuse case. "We renamed him Teddy or Theodore Wiggleton. Teddy now lives in a family with three kids and everyone adores him. He's the perfect household pet," Cynthia said. "Stories like this keep me going."

Cindy had high praise for the Court Case Dogs program. "We've been able to show that dogs are not just someone's property, that they're a pet and a member of the family. We have to be a voice for these animals that don't have voices for themselves," she said.

\*\*\*

After the meeting, Kara, Cynthia, Anisha, Ally and I made our way to Bucktown, a hip area in the city for a book signing at Kriser's All Natural Pet Foods, stopping first for a quick dinner at the Sultan's Buffet, an awesome Middle Eastern restaurant.

It was too hard to choose from the rows of delicious steaming trays of rich stewed dishes, which included a large selection of vegetarian goodies, so both Cynthia and I went with delicious falafel sandwiches and perfectly buttery, flaky baklava.

Kara was being attended to by Anisha and Ally so I could fully focus on my meal and Cynthia for a few minutes.

"Are you a vegetarian?" I asked Cynthia.

"For the most part, but I eat seafood on occasion."

"Me, too. It's kind of a new thing for me. I just didn't feel right eating farm animals when I spend so much time and energy focusing on dogs."

"It feels hypocritical, right?" Cynthia asked knowingly.

"Yes. For some reason, though, I don't really have a problem eating fish, even though I know they probably suffer, too."

"I know what you mean. I do my best to eat mostly vegetarian, but I do like my fish."

We walked the block and a half or so to Kriser's, which is a super cool, high-end store focused on quality nutrition and toys. Kim Boggs, a Safe Humane Chicago volunteer joined us, and endeared herself to Kara by playing fetch in the store. Hotel room, big green lawn, small store aisle, it didn't matter to Kara. Fetch was fetch and she dove for the ball like an Olympic volleyball champ, the bright yellow tennis ball in her mouth much more satisfying than a gold medal.

Being a Monday, store traffic was pretty slow, so Cynthia showed me a short online video about the Lifetime Bonds program while Kara continued on her rounds of fetch and affection with Kim, Anisha and Ally. The video depicted several inmates who had transitioned from being scared of dogs, usually because they had been exposed as young children to dog fighting in their neighborhoods, to being capable trainers. Not only did the program offer vital job skills to these young men, it also offered a lesson in compassion, especially when the inmates toured a Chicago animal shelter.

"These dogs are locked up, just like us," one young man said. "I want to help them when I get out."

DaShawn, who grew up afraid of dogs, really shined in the program, blossoming from a silent, almost reluctant participant to a smiling, engaged dog lover in the matter of six weeks.

"I didn't know there were so many abused dogs," he said. "I think if everyone one comes together, we can help change that."

That was touching enough, but what really struck me was when a volunteer named Janice said this, "It's so important to understand that if we're going to help animals, we need to help people, too."

She was right. I had been going through the motions when it came to education and outreach, when quite often, secretly, I was judging, or even hating people I thought were the problem. I forgot where I came from, that not everyone was as far along this path as I was. After all, I wasn't born an advocate, nor was I close to a perfect pet owner.

Just six years ago, Sam and Buster had escaped my yard several times while I was at work. I was busy, broke and not very handy, so I just kept putting it off, telling myself they were safe in our small mountain community. Then a neighbor called me about Sam showing up in his yard and scaring his family. The man told me he would call animal control the next time it happened. Finally, faced with the serious threat of losing my dog, I got the fence fixed.

In 1999, I had given my black lab Jake away for 15 months when I moved to Shanghai, China to be with my second husband, who worked there. Thankfully, my sister Heidi's in-laws took him in and I was able to get Jake back when I came home, but still. What if I hadn't been so lucky? What would I have done? Taken him to a shelter? I'd like to think not, but I'm not so sure.

When I was a teenager, I impulsively took a kitten from a family handing a litter out in front of Target and named him Pookie. This did not sit well with my sister or my best friend Jill, both roommates at the time. Jill was allergic to cats, but I wouldn't give Pookie up. Instead, I just kept him in my room. Pookie ripped the carpet something terrible, which added to the stress in our apartment. Given an ultimatum by my roommates, I had him declawed, which many advocates will tell you is totally barbaric and cruel to cats. It didn't have such a stigma at the time, but I knew that declawing took away Pookie's natural ability to scratch and protect himself, but it was either do that or give up him up. I did the best I could at the time.

As Oprah Winfrey is fond of saying, "Once you know better, you do better." I know that was true for me. It was certainly true for the young men in Lifetime Bonds. Given the proper tools, perhaps most people would choose to do the right thing by their pets, to animals in general and to one another.

# My Kind of Town

Not everyone would rise to meet the challenge, I knew, but at that moment, at that pet store, surrounded by Cynthia, Anisha, Ally and Kim, human beings that made a difference every day, and a stumpy, sweet little pit bull that was once abandoned and slotted for death, my heart opened just a little more to believe that maybe more would than wouldn't.

*"Ok, one last photo, then back to fetch!"*

## Our Own Private Idaho

What is it about eating outdoors that made food taste so good? Or was it just the home-cooking of my mother and some long-overdue family time that made a simple meal of salmon, salad and rice so delicious?

Kara and I made it to camp with my parents at their RV spot in West Yellowstone after three days of marathon driving. Making up the miles across the Midwest required a lot of caffeine and good music. Still, once the first few hundred miles went by and the caffeine buzz wore off, it became a test of your will. Watching the GPS, I'd note, "OK, we're halfway through, only 250, 200, 150, 100 miles to go…" my eyes starting to droop with each passing off-ramp.

I'd look at Kara, snoozing peacefully, her little pink snout on the console, her breath on my forearm, with envy, because I too wanted to nap, as well as with gratitude, for being such a trooper. All she required was a potty and fetch break every 100 miles or so. I'd pat Kara's booty or rub her soft golden fur whenever I felt a little crazy from the unceasing asphalt, an instant mood enhancer.

Somewhere across Iowa my cell phone rang. It was Michele Buttelman, my boss at The Signal. After my trip with Loren, I had been promoted to a full-time assistant features editor. They had been so kind as to let me take this trip and file two stories from the road each week.

Unfortunately, Michele was not calling with good news. "We're having major budget issues and it looks like you're going to be cut back to part-time," she said.

"What? Why me?"

"You know how it is, features is always one of the first departments to be cut. We had to let Stephen go completely," Michele said. Stephen Peeples was the online content editor, a former Rhino Records PR executive who had hobnobbed with musicians for decades and was even nominated for a Grammy for writing the liner notes to a John Lennon album. He had been a fixture at The Signal.

"Wow, that really sucks," I said. "So, how many hours are we talking about?"

"Probably 25 a week. I'm really sorry."

"That means no benefits either. That's just great."

"Michelle, you do a great job and I love you. This is no reflection on your work."

"Yeah, yeah, I do such a great job, this is how I get rewarded. I feel really honored." Michele and I were like an old married couple after working together for seven years. There was no point in holding back. She knew I was pissed.

"If I could change it I would," Michele said.

"I know. I'm just bummed."

The endless cornfields of Iowa swished by as I was consumed by thoughts, none positive. The news wasn't a huge surprise. The Signal, like many newspapers, was suffering due to competition from online media and the relentless recession. That's why I hoped "Pit Stops" would turn into something that could sustain me financially, but unless a miracle happened by the time I returned home, that didn't look likely. There had been no national publicity, no Oprah Winfrey show. I had only sold half the books I had wanted to. Animal welfare organizations were not knocking down my door to offer me a communications job.

"Oh, Kara," I said as she hazily glanced at me through droopy lips. "What am I going to do?" We were parked under the awning of the world's largest truck stop in Walcott, Iowa. It was a foggy day, grey and depressing, just like my mood.

Kara's answer to everything that ailed you was playing ball, which we did on an enormous lawn as big rigs whirred by on the highway above. It did, I admit, brighten my spirits. So did a visit with my aunt Marla on our way to Lincoln, Nebraska. Marla lives in Omaha and treated us to a sandwich at Jimmy John's, a chain I'd never heard of before. I had a sandwich with on a fresh, fluffy French roll, filled lots of cheese, avocado and crunchy veggies, while Kara enjoyed a little stretch time the patio.

The next day we did our longest stretch, 620 miles to Casper, Wyoming. Loud music was definitely in order. I rediscovered several of my favorite CD's - Cheap Trick's "Live at Budokan," Jane's Addiction's "Nothing's Shocking," Green Day's "American Idiot," and The

Foo Fighters' "Colour and The Shape" – singing along loudly, playing air guitar or drums. In this ADD age of Twitter, iPods and satellite radio, it seemed almost decadent listening to entire albums. Despite the racket, Kara would just raise her eyebrow, the creases in her forehead deepening for a moment, before drifting back into slumber. No judgment (I am not the best singer). No calls to turn it down or put on different CD. She was the best.

I thought our trip from Casper to West Yellowstone would only be 175 miles, but I found out from my father that it was closer to 350. These were not easy miles, either, but country highways followed by two-lane mountain roads overrun by tourists. Traffic slowed to a crawl in some spots. A buffalo ambled along the passenger side of the car, where Kara continued to sleep, not even looking up at the large, fuzzy beast. People were lined up the road a ways, so I knew an interesting creature was in view. Sure enough, a mama bear and her two cubs were wandering slowly up a rolling hill, surrounded by more bison. I smiled and kept driving.

*"Hey guys, is that a squirrel?"*

## Our Own Private Idaho

My parents bought a used 34' fifth wheel RV a few years ago and travel across the country with it. Their two dogs, Annie, a small Benji-like terrier mix and Sammy, a 90-lb fluffy golden mutt, love the RV life. Sammy, however, does not always love other dogs, so Kara was relegated to her crate, so big we called it the doggy condo, while we stayed there. Everyone was safe and at peace this way. Especially Aunt Michelle, who still needed to master some pack leader skills, but was reluctant to do so with someone else's dog.

I took Kara out for long games of fetch throughout the day, which the frigid temperatures allowed for. We played in a desolate stretch of grass and logs. There were signs warning of grizzly bears, but somehow this didn't bother me like the idea of being near alligators. I was a mountain girl, after all. Mammals were just a lot less scary to me than primitive reptiles. Like I could somehow reason with one better or possibly scare it away. Crazy, I know.

Kara was in heaven, running, jumping, rolling to catch the ball, dropping it at my feet. Such an athlete. It was funny, I didn't see Kara's physicality, her muscular stature, her block head, her immense strength, unless we were playing fetch. Otherwise, I just saw her gentle spirit, her soft fur, her smooshy face, her silly pointy ears, her wiggly booty, her innocent, loving eyes. Like most pit bulls, Kara is a marshmallow soul wrapped in a tough-dog suit.

"Zzzzzzz..."

Afterwards, while Kara snoozed, I relaxed under my mother's loving care. She made up for some of my less-than-healthy road food choices by serving me salads, salmon, rice, sautéed vegetables, fresh fruit and yogurt.

During the day, Kara and I napped together on the surprisingly comfortable queen bed vacated by my parents. Kara the world-class snuggler burrowed against me, reaching around to lick my face, before she'd breathe a final sigh and drift off, followed shortly by me.

We left on Saturday morning for Idaho Falls, where my folks live. Kara and I had a signing that afternoon at the Idaho Falls Animal Shelter.

My parents had adopted Annie there. She was found as a stray in a nearby town and had just been picked up by animal control when my dad came into the shelter. Annie turned on the charm, coming up to the kennel door and licking my father's hand. They've been smitten with one another ever since.

Danyelle Harker, who worked Saturdays at the shelter and fosters pit bulls through Boise Bully Breed Rescue, had put the event together. We are Facebook friends.

Decked out in her blingy "Kara" scarf, Kara quickly launched into her ambassador role, welcoming guests, including a father and his two young sons that engulfed her with hugs.

It was so refreshing to see a parent that didn't buy into the pit bull bias. He simply asked me if Kara was friendly, and once I assured him she was, the kids were set free to interact with her like any other dog. They were rewarded with a succession of Kara kisses, which caused the kids to shriek with delight.

It was a fairly busy day at the shelter. Volunteers Shirlene Tomchak and Monica Wright were taking dogs outside and snapping photos to post them on Facebook and network for rescue. I'd hear one say it was time to go, yet a half hour later, they will still there, interacting with potential adopters or cat testing a dog. They didn't leave until 6 p.m., when we did.

The Idaho Falls Shelter has a live release rate, a combination of owner reclamations, adoptions and rescues, of 90 percent. This was an increase of about 10 percent from the previous year, which Danyelle credited to Shirlene and Monica.

"Those ladies are amazing," Danyelle said. "They've saved so many of our animals. Sometimes they take seven to 10 at a time out to rescues."

Mya, an orange and white pit bull mix, was a favorite of shelter staff and volunteers. The sweet young dog had hanging teats, like Kara once did, and a playful, yet mellow spirit.

"She was brought in as a stray with her puppy. The puppy got adopted, but Mya's been here for a while," Danyelle said sadly. "I so want for her to get a home. She's a wonderful dog."

An unnamed four month old Shepherd puppy, who was so terrified he barely looked up from the floor, was sitting on Monica's lap. Mya came over, sniffed the puppy and began playing with him. Slowly, but surely, the puppy's tiny tail began to wag.

As I watched this scene, a young man came in and spoke to the front desk clerk. "I need to surrender my dog. I'm being deployed soon."

"Can't you find someone to take care of your dog while you're gone?" the clerk asked kindly.

"No, I can't," he said. The man paid the surrender fee, walked out and returned holding a young black male pit bull, which squirmed in his arms. They followed the clerk to the kennel area, the barking growing louder as they entered. A few minutes later, the man emerged, red-faced, wiping the tears from his cheeks, and left again.

I looked at Danyelle and shook my head. "At least he had the decency to cry." So much for my newfound compassion.

"Yeah, it seemed like he really cared. He had only adopted that dog a few months ago. He didn't know he was going to be deployed," she replied. "His dog is young and very cute. Hopefully, we can find him a home."

Danyelle's assessment was not only comforting, it reminded me not to judge people so harshly. That man was doing the best that he could. What could I do under the same circumstances?

George, a blue-eyed cattle dog mix, was one of the day's success stories. He was going home with a couple that clearly adored him, to the delight of Danyelle, Monica and Shirlene. George had been there the longest of any dog to that point.

"Have a nice life, George," I called out as he was leaving.

## Pit Stops 2

*Danyelle Harker says goodbye to Spike*

"Oh, he will," his new mom assured me. "He will."

Spike, a male pit bull mix, was not so lucky. A court case dog, Spike had escaped his yard and killed a neighbor's Schnauzer.

While this was not automatic cause for euthanization in Idaho, his owner had signed the paperwork for Spike to be put down. Danyelle brought him out to lobby area, plying Spike with treats and wet food, playing with him on his last day on earth.

"It breaks my heart," she said, her eyes misting up. "Spike's a good dog. If only his owner would have had him fixed and kept him under control and trained him. It didn't have to end this way."

\*\*\*

On Sunday, Kara and I slept in before I headed off for a recovery meeting. The day was largely open to relax. My parents were hosting a party in our honor that evening with their eclectic group of friends, many from a political group called Drinking Liberally.

My dad grilled bratwursts and barbeque chicken, which I had to admit, were tempting. I didn't succumb, though. I had remained meat-free for the whole trip so far and wasn't going to give up so close to home. This was not an easy task, let me tell you, especially going through the south. There were a lot of bean burritos along the way. But it felt really good to hold on to my newfound diet.

Kym Lewis, a fellow author, and Dawn Browning were keen to meet Kara. Both are dog lovers. Kym and her husband Doug have fostered dogs for years, while Dawn in particular loves pit bulls.

"What a cutie!" Dawn exclaimed when she saw Kara, calling her over. Kara lapped her face, to Dawn's delight. "Oh, I miss having a pit bull. They're just the best dogs."

"I'm just going to say that my dog Gilligan is best dog in the world, but Kara is right up there," Kym said. "She's just wonderful."

I agreed. Kara was amazing. I trusted her gentle soul implicitly, on or off leash. It shocked me that Kara was in the shelter, bound for death, until Carol, then Kyle, stepped in to save her. I could envision those beautiful eyes looking up at a technician holding a life-ending needle and it made my heart hurt for the millions of Karas who don't get out alive.

***

It's one thing to have friends, family and even total strangers commend Kara, quite another when you get professional validation. After leaving Idaho Falls, Kara and I had lunch with Julie Anderson, a dog behaviorist in Boise. Julie, another Facebook friend, fosters pit bulls through Boise Bully Breed Rescue and had adopted 18-20 dogs over the last year and a half.

She, her husband Rich and their two kids met us at a strip mall Baja Fresh (finally, a taste of home), along with Charlie Brown, a ten-week old pit bull puppy they were fostering. Kara immediately gravitated to the puppy, sniffing and licking him.

Julie bought me a veggie burrito stuffed full of grilled peppers, onions and black beans, cheese and salsa. Healthy and heavenly. We ate on the shaded patio while the rest of the Anderson clan ran an errand. Kara lounged in the shade at Julie's feet.

"Is it going to be hard for you to give Kara back?" she asked.

"Yes, but at least I know she's going to a great home," I replied. "How about you? Is it challenging to foster so much?"

"As hard as it is, there is nothing so rewarding. People always say they could never do it because they couldn't give the dogs up. But I have found giving them up is the easy part," Julie answered. "By the time you put in so much effort and love to get them adopted, that moment when they connect with a family and you see them safe and happy, sometimes for the first time, the tears come from joy not pain in letting them go."

The dogs have given the Anderson family a cause to bond over. According to Julie, her husband and daughter worked just as hard as she did when a new foster came into the home. "It was my idea, yet my whole family pulls together to make it our project. I see it make my kids more compassionate and responsible. I am very blessed."

Fostering also puts Rich in a new light. "To be honest, I am never more in love with my husband than when I see him giving up his after work relax time to take a high-energy foster dog on a bike ride," Julie said with a big smile.

I knew what she meant. Whenever I saw a man be nice to an animal, it instantly elevated and made them more attractive in my eyes. Much like what I imagine most women, mothers or those that wanted to be, would feel watching a man with a baby. Kindness is sexy.

Julie shared her experiences training dog owners and the methods she imparts as a behaviorist. Many of these methods, such as making your dog work for their food and presenting calm, assertive energy under any situation, Wayde does instinctively. It's funny, because I'm the big dog lover in the house, but definitely not the best pack leader.

After lunch, when the Andersons returned, Julie did a little trick with Kara. She held a couple of crushed dog biscuits out in her hand and closed it whenever Kara approached. After about 15 seconds, Kara ignored the biscuits in Julie's outstretched hand.

"Wow," Julie said. "They say dogs are very intelligent if they ignore the treats after 55 seconds or less. She did it in under 30 seconds."

"She did it in under 10 seconds, mom," her son cried out.

"She's a smart dog, for sure," I said, a proud auntie. "Kara's mom wants to make her a CGC dog and take her into schools to educate kids."

"She's perfect for it. Kara has an amazing temperament and is very intelligent. I bet she'd pass her CGC training today."

Julie was kneeling on the ground, holding Kara close. She looked up at me, her kind blue eyes pensive. "Can you imagine the utter tragedy it would have been if the shelter had put Kara down?"

*"Really, I'm a smart dog?"*

# Setting the Example

The time had come for me to say goodbye to Kara, even if we weren't leaving for two more days. We were lightly napping in our Reno hotel room, watching TV with nothing on the schedule. The next day we had plans to tour Nevada Humane Society and have a signing, too. Since it would be so hectic and our last day was focused on the long drive home, my idea was to get my emotional breakdown out of the way. What can I say? The Great American Road Trip created an intense bond that was hard to break.

Holding her close, my tears rained down on Kara's fuzzy head. "Kare Bear, thank you for being my friend. Thank you for putting up with me. Thank you for being such a great ambassador for pit bulls."

*"Nappy time..."*

She turned around to face me, her forehead creased, those beautiful, crazy ears pointing to the heavens. "You've been the best buddy anyone could ever ask for. I'm going to miss you so much, but I know you're going to the best place possible with Mama Kyle."

Her gold eyes looking into mine, Kara just kept kissing my face as I cried.

# Setting the Example

I was trying to even out my breathing and calm down when the phone rang. It was my friend Ronni in Pine Mountain Club. Part of me didn't want to answer it, but I wanted to see what was going on back home.

"Hello?"

"Michelle?"

"Hey, Ronni, how are you?"

"Good, how are you?"

"I'm sad," I said and started bawling all over again. "It's just going to be so hard to part with Kara. She's been my buddy for all this time." My nose was starting to run. I was pathetic, but couldn't stop. "I really love her..." my voice trailed off into a whimper.

"Oh, Michelle," Ronni said, sympathetically. Ronni was a dog lover, she had adopted her two dogs from Bow-Wows & Meows, but she wasn't an activist. She didn't have time, being a divorced mom with a full-time job. I'm sure my doggy angst was something she just couldn't relate to and might even be thought of as frivolous in her world. Still, Ronni tried to assuage me. "You will be sad for a while, but think of all the good times you had together. You two had a really cool trip. "

"I know. You're right. I'm a weirdo, huh?" I asked, sniffling. "Well, enough about me and my trauma. How are you?"

"Well, I have some news…I'm getting married!" she said breathlessly. "Jim asked me a few days ago and I said yes."

"Wow. That's great. Congratulations. Here I am going on and on about a dog and you're getting married! I'm really happy for you. I want all the details."

"Yeah, I'm happy, too," Ronni said, launching into the location, the dress, the ceremony.

I listened and held Kara close, determined to get out of my melancholy and back into the real world that awaited me once I returned home. Ronni's wedding was something to look forward to. My uncertain future, however, was not. I sighed, snuggled into Kara even more, and listened to my happy friend. Tomorrow was another day.

\*\*\*

If you're a YouTube fan and an animal lover, there's a good chance you may have seen the "Adoption Entrance Dance" video posted by Nevada Humane Society (113,000 hits and counting). While the shelter rings a bell every time a pet gets adopted, for this video, the staff and volunteers performed an elaborate, enthusiastic dance down the lobby's hallway when Cooper, a lab mix, finds his forever home. The video closes with "We get excited about adoptions."

They should. In 2007, Nevada Humane Society launched an ambitious no-kill initiative to make Washoe County, Nevada one of the safest communities in the United States for homeless animals. By the end of that year, 92 percent of all dogs and 78 percent of all cats found loving new homes, were reclaimed or, in the case of feral cats, were adopted as barn cats or returned to their habitats. Adoptions increased 53 percent for dogs and 84 percent for cats, while euthanizations decreased by 51 percent for dogs and 52 percent for cats.

"The only reasons we euthanize are due to illness or injury for which there is no cure or treatment or if a dog is too aggressive and poses a risk. Neither decision is made lightly," said Diane Blankenburg, community programs and development director for NHS.

Diane was giving Kara and me a tour of the shelter, a large, impressive single-story building that housed up to 400 cats and 200 dogs at any given time. Animal control was located in the building next door and took the strays, while NHS cared for the owner surrenders and any strays that were not reclaimed.

"Right now, moving and an inability to afford a pet are the top reasons people are surrendering their pets," Diane said.

In addition to the beautiful shelter facilities, NHS offered a help desk that fielded thousands of calls each month, plus a pet food pantry and free spay/neuter and other medical assistance at their in-house clinic to low-income residents. NHS had really innovative enrichment programs, too, such as Hiking Buddies, which allowed trained volunteers to take out dogs for a long trek in the beautiful surrounding mountains. They also built a strong foster network that took care of another 300 pets, according to Diane.

Out of 10,000 dogs and cats that came into NHS over the past year, 9,668 were adopted. During our tour, the adoption bell rang several times.

## Setting the Example

"That's awesome!" I exclaimed the first time it rang.

Diane smiled. "Marketing is a big part of it. We had a special on small dogs here about four months ago. Adoption fees were only $50, which included spay or neuter, vaccinations and a microchip. We regularly have specials where pets are free to $50."

To encourage adoptions that month, NHS had partnered with the ASPCA for a free "Adopt a Cat" promotion. We passed through the lobby, which was lined with endless rows of metal cat cages. Down the hallway, the sunny yellow walls had clear glass cubbies featuring even more cats. Young ones, older ones, black ones, white ones and every color in between. Their cages were well appointed with hammocks, food dishes and tiny litter boxes, but my heart went out to them. Yes, I'm a dog person, but I love cats, too.

There were a lot of fuzzy Persians that reminded me of Sugar Butt. As we stopped to chat, a young Pookie doppelganger stuck his little paw out of the bars and grasped on to my finger. I stroked his back through the narrow bars. "I hope you find a home soon," I said before reluctantly pulling my hand back.

Kara was very interested in the cats, her ears standing up like little

*"Are you our new person?"*

## Pit Stops 2

*"Did you see that cat, Trish?"*

radars, but she didn't make any aggressive moves towards them. I was so proud of her. She was wearing her bling-y Kara scarf and attracting the attention of every employee and volunteer within a 30-foot radius.

Volunteer Trish Hafely was one of them. She rushed to Kara and got on her knees for some serious pitty love. Trish sat down on the linoleum floor and held Kara close, both of them lost in mutual affection. While she didn't have a pit of her own, Trish adored the breed, especially after helping her sister raise a pit bull named Miko.

"We have a lab and a Rottweiler, so I do know what it's like to have a misunderstood dog. Even when my dog was a pup, people would cross the street," Trish said.

She had volunteered at NHS since December 2010, after an early retirement (which the pretty brunette did not look old enough to do). NHS was fortunate to have more than a thousand volunteers at their organization, though Trish was particularly passionate.

"What I enjoy most about volunteering with dogs is seeing the smiles on their faces, the wags of their tails. I enjoy taking them on a nice, leisurely walk. I provide them with time in the grass to roll around and I give a lot of kisses and hugs," Trish said. "I tell them they are a good dog and that I love them."

Funny, I did the same thing whenever I volunteered at Brittany. It may not be a home, but when a dog's at a shelter, they should be treated like family. I was glad Trish felt the same way.

## Setting the Example

One difficulty of volunteering in a shelter with a high population of pit bulls, Trish told me, was dealing with the public's prejudice. As she walks one of NHS' many bully breed residents back to the kennel, Trish often hears: "Why are there so many pit bulls in here?" or "I don't like pit bulls." It made her heart ache, but Trish tried to educate people whenever she could and help them overcome the harsh media stereotype.

'Sometimes I strike up a conversation, 'Oh, have you ever had a pit bull?' Most say no and it's usually followed by, 'You hear so many bad stories about those dogs.' In truth, each dog that comes into the shelter must pass an extensive evaluation and it is apparent these pit bulls do it with no problem. That in and of itself should speak volumes," Trish said with palpable frustration.

Unfortunately, reason didn't always work. The dog kennels, which were quite spacious and very clean with guillotine doors that allowed indoor/outdoor access, contained a high percentage of pit bull type dogs. They greeted us with barks or wagging tails, as did the smaller contingent of adorable little dogs and some large mixed breeds. Each kennel noted if a dog was a senior or had been there a long time.

*Sign at Nevada Humane Society*

There were also bright, eye-catching signs hanging in the hallways boasting the virtues of seniors and pit bulls. As we walked past, an older fluffy black chow mix lifted his head briefly to observe the commotion before settling back in for a nap.

"He's one of our longest residents, he's been here about two years," Diane told me sadly.

Therein lays the rub of "no-kill" shelters. It sounds like nirvana in theory, but many animals end up living years or their entire lives in a kennel as a result. Then the public and animal welfare groups like PETA decry the cruelty of this "warehousing" scenario. Ideally, more people would be open to adopting an older dog or a pit bull or an adult cat. But ask any rescuer or shelter volunteer and they'll tell you, the puppies and young, small white "fluffies" are the first to be adopted, while the rest can really struggle (yes, even cute little kittens) to find homes.

At NHS, the volunteers made extra efforts to get old-timers, primarily bully breeds, out. Trish noted that when dogs are at NHS more than three months, volunteers will pitch in to run an advertisement to showcase them to the public. "Many pit bulls have been placed solely on the efforts of the volunteers. We advocate for them and try to be their voice."

It was lunchtime, so Kara was taken to an office for babysitting while Diane and I went out for a bite. She drove us in her well-worn SUV to a small restaurant located in an industrial building. It was called The Wet Hen and the chef was the boyfriend of Kimberly Chandler, communications manager at NHS. The café-like interior was very homey and welcoming, as was the menu, which featured soups, sandwiches, quiches and several vegetarian selections. I opted for the potato leek soup and a grilled cheese sandwich. The latter had a tangy streak of Dijon mustard that cut through the richness of the cheese, a gourmet trick I planned to try at home.

With her long silver hair, elegant bearing, and clear passion for the animals, Diane reminded me of a younger Jane Goodall. Diane had worked at the Best Friends Network before taking the position at NHS in 2007. She was also the mother to three adopted labs, all boys. Diane was full of fantastic information on the ins and outs of working in animal welfare. There were definitely ups and downs, even when you're as successful as NHS, which was a national model for the no-kill movement.

"What's the toughest part of your job?" I asked Diane.

"Doing so much with limited resources...and knowing that so many animals are dependent upon us to be saved," she said.

I imagined that would be a tough cross to bear, especially seeing hundreds of homeless pets on a daily basis. Like most of the staff at NHS, Diane didn't just put in a 40-hour week, either. There were fundraising events, adoption events, and the never-ending emails and phone calls. Did I really want to do this for a living? It would be hard, but I wanted to give it a shot. Hopefully, a group like NHS in Southern California would be willing to give a very passionate volunteer like me a shot to turn pro.

\*\*\*

Kara and I reunited in time for the book signing, which was set up at the far end of the lobby, by the entrance to the dog kennels. Someone had designed a sign with our photos on it and placed it on the table, along with juice and cookies for the crowds. A line had begun to form, which shocked me. Bonney Brown, the director at NHS, had written a review on "Pit Stops" in the local paper, so it attracted attention beyond the volunteers and staff who were always my biggest customers.

Trish and several other volunteers were hanging out in the hallway, showcasing several of the available pit bulls. NHS was offering a $5 adoption special, good on any bully breed, that day. During a lull, I went over and met them. There were many wonderful dogs vying for attention, but one stuck out.

His name was Cyrus and he was a sweet, handsome deaf pit bull who'd been there 25 months, making him the longest-term canine resident. Cyrus was adopted once, but returned when his new person couldn't deal with the requirements of a deaf dog. Really, all it took was a little human training, learning hand signals instead of using one's voice to communicate. Cyrus would make a wonderful companion for a patient person willing to put in the time.

"He's my favorite," Trish told me as she rubbed his black and white coat. "I wish I could take him myself."

"I know how that is, Trish. I had the same thing with Loren. Broke my heart."

## Pit Stops 2

At day's end, I sold 30 books and felt like a rock star. So did Kara, who was mobbed from the start. She just shined in the spotlight. Kara would make a perfect therapy dog. I was grateful she was going home to Kyle, someone that would let her reach her full potential.

"So, how'd you do?" Diane asked me as the signing came to a close.

"Great, it was the most successful event of the whole trip. Thank you so much!"

"I'm so glad. Thank you for coming out," Diane said. "If you're not too tired, would you like to have dinner? There's a great place on the waterfront with really delicious food. We have events there all the time, so it's dog-friendly, with a patio for Kara."

Though I was burnt out, I couldn't resist. The Wild River Grille, surrounded by the shimmering Truckee River and the sparkling lights of the Reno strip, was everything Diane promised. Live contemporary pop and jazz played while Kara lapped up a grilled chicken breast. Diane and I split several appetizers, including a delectable crab and salmon cake, and never ran out of conversation. We clinked our glasses together (mine water, hers wine), a toast to a successful day and the perfect end to a long journey.

*\*\*\**

Steep mountainous highways scare the crap out of me, especially when the landscape that surrounds it is distractingly beautiful. Visions of sailing thousands of feet down towards a fiery end a la "Thelma and Louise" torment me. Such was the case of Interstate 80, where the blue skies, tall redwood trees and gorgeous mountains of the Sierra Nevada beckoned my gaze as I barreled down the road, trying to get home as quickly as possible without getting a ticket or in an accident. Seeing the Donner Pass sign didn't ease my anxiety. Well, at least it wasn't winter. I hated driving in snow, though I was used to it after 10 years of living in Pine Mountain Club. Doing so on a quiet, two-lane back road versus a major thoroughfare with big rigs in the mix is very different, however.

"Focus, Sathe, focus," I told myself, forcing my eyes to stay on the asphalt. I patted Kara's booty for reassurance. She looked up at me as a child might from a long nap, almost uncomprehending of what was going on outside her dream world. Kara's eyes went from half open to closed, as she lowered her massive head back on the fuzzy pink blanket and sighed.

It was going to be weird driving without my sidekick, to not meet her gentle gaze in the seat next to me anymore. It takes 21 days to form a habit and we had been together about 40, so Kara withdrawal was definitely in my near future. I, too, sighed and took a long sip off my Starbucks green tea lemonade, sustenance for the trip ahead.

The 400 miles were long, but we made it to Castaic Shelter, our designated meeting place with Kyle, by mid-afternoon. I pulled up in the parking lot and texted Kyle. Kara sprung to life, sitting up and looking about. The faint barks of dogs wafting over the full blast air-conditioner had caught her attention.

She looked at me, golden eyes blinking, pink blanket in fuzzy disarray. I leaned over and exhaled, burrowing into my buff little friend for what would be the last time. "We made it. We did it," I pulled away and looked in her sweet golden eyes. "Welcome home, Kara. You're safe. You will be loved for the rest of your life."

I was starting to blubber. Kara cocked her head, then leaned over and licked my face, which made me cry harder. Where was Kyle?

"I'm going to go find your mom, Pookie La La," I told Kara. "Be right back." Leaving the A/C on, I got out of the car and into the stifling heat. Down the rows of kennels, I saw a couple of volunteers, noteworthy from their burgundy shirts, moving towards me. It was Hsiawen Hull and Clare Storey.

I was waving wildly from the fence, sobbing and feeling like an idiot. Both were friends and followed our adventures on the road – Clare had seen us off at Kyle's house – so I knew they'd understand.

"Welcome home, Michelle," Hsiawen said, giving me a hug. He was one of the few male volunteers I'd seen in rescue, which tends to be about 95 percent women. Hsiawen was a very compassionate person, though his usual demeanor was somewhat impassive. "Aww, don't cry..."

"I'm just sad...it's been a long trip...and I...don't know...," I said, my nose starting to run, which I wiped on my hand. Very classy. I was already disheveled, hair up in a haphazard bun and sweaty from the drive. This was not helping. "I'm just going to miss Kara."

Clare engulfed me in a big hug, before pulling back and looking me square in the eye.

"Are you OK?" I loved Clare's proper English accent, it was very comforting. I nodded and she slipped an arm around my shoulder. "I'm very proud of you. Good going!"

Kyle finally walked over from the shelter office. "You did it, Michelle," she said, holding me tight for many moments. She pulled back and I could see Kyle's eyes glistening. "How's my girl?"

"Come here and see," I said, making my way to the passenger side of the RAV. Once she saw Kyle, Kara practically jumped up and down. I opened the door and she sprung onto the ground, hugging Kyle's legs in earnest.

Kyle bent down and lovingly stroked Kara's head and body, then gave her a visual once-over, looking slightly awe-struck. "She looks great, Michelle, really great. Don't you, Kara?"

She pronounced it Car-a, while I always said Care-A. I just considered it my auntie's prerogative.

"Yes, she does," I said proudly.

"It's like she got a tummy tuck," Kyle said. We both laughed. It was true, Kara had slimmed down considerably. You could barely tell she had been a breeder anymore.

"She's a great dog, just the best," I said wistfully. "I'm going to miss her a lot."

Kyle stood up, sympathetically patted me on the shoulder and handed me Kara's leash.

"Let me go get the car. We're going home!" she said to Kara, whose nub wagged in earnest at the notion or just at the sound of Kyle's voice.

This was it. I lifted Kara into the passenger side of Kyle's SUV. She had mastered getting out of the car, but it didn't look like getting in by herself would ever be in Kara's future, unless Kyle invested in a low-rider. She was just too short.

"Bye, Kare Bear. Be a good girl," I said, rubbing her head through the window. Kara's tongue was hanging out, a big grin across her face. She looked at me, then Kyle, and settled down into her seat, which I had laid the prophetic pink blanket on. Kara was an old pro at shotgun now.

"Thanks, Michelle," Kyle said. "You'll always be her auntie."

## Setting the Example

I kissed Kara's head for the last time and stifled a sniffle.

"We'll see you soon, OK?"

I nodded. The window rolled up and the SUV drove away. I watched until it disappeared from view and started to cry again. Kara was truly on her way home, yet I was more lost than ever.

*"Bye, Aunt Michelle.*
*Thanks for the trip!"*

# Finding My Way

It was an uncharacteristically warm day in February, even for Pacoima, a largely Latino community in the San Fernando Valley. I was standing in the parking lot at Restaurant El Indio, which featured a striking mural of the actor Danny Trejo of "Machete" fame. The real Danny Trejo was standing just feet away from me, interacting with local dog owners that had come for the free spay/neuter clinic with AngelDogs Foundation, my new employer.

After many months of limbo at The Signal, where I was basically told that I had no future and my part-time hours would not be extended, my luck finally changed. Lisa Tipton, the director of AngelDogs Foundation, found out that I was looking for full-time work and offered me a job as an outreach coordinator.

Lisa was unconcerned that I didn't have a college degree and that my only experience in animal welfare up to this point had been as a volunteer. "I think you're the right person to join our team and move us forward," she told me.

Mark Tipton, Lisa's husband, was a positive reinforcement dog trainer in the Santa Clarita Valley. The three of us had gotten to know one another over a series of lunches before and after the book tour. The Tiptons privately rescued deaf dogs from shelters all over the country, many of which were white Staffordshire Terrier or Dogo Argentino mixes, and had plans to open a rescue facility in Acton in the near future.

As much as she loved rescue, however, spay and neuter was Lisa's reigning passion. She had started off as a volunteer for a spay/neuter clinic in Los Angeles and gave up a successful medical billing career to launch AngelDogs Foundation in 2009. Since then, the mobile clinic had fixed more 15,000 dogs and cats across Southern California. "We're not going to rescue our way out of this mess," Lisa has told me many times and I agree.

So, in January of 2012, I went from being a journalist to writing grants, press releases, event planning and fundraising. The event in Pacoima was the result of a collaboration with Dogs on Death Row, which sponsored the spay/neuter clinic, and K9 Compassion, which promoted the free services by having Danny speak at a local high school a few weeks prior.

At 7 a.m., I pulled up and there was Danny in a leather jacket and a baseball cap. He shook my hand and greeted me warmly, then commenced to set up tables and welcome everyone. Cars and trucks had started trickling in, families with one to four dogs, some on leashes. Others came in laundry baskets or were held by their owners.

A few people cried as their dogs were carried onboard the clinic truck by staff. "She's my baby," one woman said to me as I reassured that her dog was in good hands. "I just can't stand the thought of my baby being hurt, but I know this is the right thing to do."

A beautiful grey pit bull caught my eye. She was being walked by a young man as his younger brother and mother sat on the sidelines, filling out paperwork. "That is a beautiful dog," I said, leaning down to pet the exuberant young dog. "What's her name?"

"Ruby. We got her from a neighbor," he told me.

"That's great that you're getting her fixed. There are too many pit bulls in shelters already. There doesn't need to be any more puppies brought into the world."

"Yeah, I know," the young man, Ignacio, replied. "That's why we're here. I don't want to breed my Ruby. I just want her to be happy and enjoy life."

A huge grin broke out on my face. "That's awesome, Ignacio. I wish everyone did the same thing for their dog. You're a smart young man."

He smiled back. "Thanks."

As the day wore on, throngs of people flooded in and out of the parking lot, including Los Angeles City Councilmember Richard Alarcon, who sponsored the mandatory spay neuter ordinance in the city. He was a childhood friend of Danny's. Both had grown up within blocks of the restaurant.

Spanish music was blaring and the sun beat down, causing everyone to take off their jackets and Danny his shirt. The large, dark tattoos all over his chest and back, plus the myriad scars on his face, gave Danny a menacing look onscreen, but he was far from it in real life. Earlier in the day, I had seen the man pick up dog poop for a total stranger. He was a very kind human being.

## Pit Stops 2

As I took pictures, I met all sorts of people, including a couple who had adopted their pit mix Bodhi from a woman who was losing her home and listed the dog for free on Craigslist. They had heard about the event on TV and came without an appointment in hopes to get Bodhi fixed. AngelDogs Foundation fit Bodhi in, despite already having 50 dogs scheduled, which was a very hectic day.

"Thank you so much, what you're doing is wonderful," the woman told me after I introduced myself. "We needed to get Bodhi fixed but we just can't afford it right now."

I took her hand into my own for a second. "Thank you for rescuing Bodhi. He probably wouldn't have fared well at a shelter. He's a beautiful dog."

"Yeah, we love him. He sleeps in bed with us," she revealed shyly.

"He's a very lucky boy."

Suddenly, she hugged me. "We're just so grateful for what you all are doing."

Returning the impromptu embrace, I said, "Well, we're grateful you saved Bodhi."

Back by the truck, a woman and her husband were speaking in Spanish with Anthony, a vet tech. In the man's arms was a gorgeous tan and white male pit bull puppy, about three months old, with clearly visible testicles.

"Anthony, are they going to get him fixed?" I asked.

Rapid-fire Spanish was exchanged. The husband's head keep shaking no, while the wife was shaking hers yes and looking pleadingly at us.

"She wants to, but he doesn't," Anthony said.

Lisa came over to see what was going on and attempted to convince the man in her limited Spanish to get the dog neutered. He kept shaking his head.

I spotted Danny out of the corner of my eye, talking to a crowd of fans, and bee-lined over to him. I tapped his shoulder. "Danny, there's a man over here that doesn't want to get his pit puppy fixed. Can you talk to him?"

He didn't hesitate. "Yeah, sure, where is he?"

"Follow me…" I said. Danny walked right up to the man, shook his hand, then grabbed the puppy, holding it up and making baby talk

Finding My Way

in his rough, gravelly voice. Danny handed the dog back to the wife and engaged the man directly, maintaining eye contact.

While I couldn't understand what was actually being said, it seemed to be working. The man went from shaking his head no to shrugging his shoulders to giving a resigned nod of his head within the space of a minute.

Danny slapped the man on the back repeatedly, made several loud proclamations in Spanish and handed Lisa the puppy. She quickly, triumphantly whisked the tiny dog up the steps of the truck to be fixed.

Smiling, I walked back into the crowd. One person at a time.

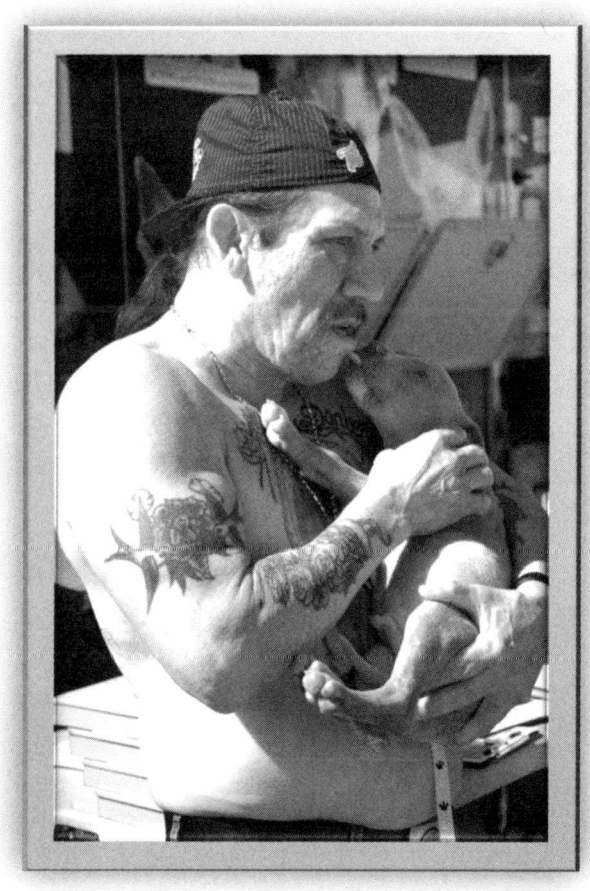

*"I'm getting fixed? Oh, thank you!"*

# Epilogue

*Kara and Kyle*

Kara settled very happily into the Harris home. She is now a Canine Good Citizen and Kyle is working on making Kara a therapy dog to help young children learn how to read. In March, 2012, Kara was bit by a rattlesnake. Thanks to Kyle's quick action, she made a full recovery. The Harris household continues to foster shelter dogs. Poppy, a young female pit bull recovered from a fighting ring, was nursed backed to health from a serious case of mange and malnutrition as was Peggy, a blue breeding bully. Kyle and I have become close friends and Kara usually accompanies us on outings.

Booker the puppy is now a massive 80-pounder. Carol Rock and her husband, Frank, love him wholeheartedly. Carol has become a passionate advocate for the breed, defending them against negative, untruthful media attacks through her work as a journalist for KHTS, a Santa Clarita Valley radio station. Her primary targets have been the deputies on the radio for the LA County Sheriff's Department. Carol's theory is "one watch commander at a time."

## Epilogue & Resources

Animal Rescue New Orleans celebrated its 7,000th adoption in the summer of 2012, adopting out more than 1,000 pets a year since it opened in 2006.

Ashley Owen Hill officially received non-profit status for Lucky Dog Rescue and continues to save dogs from all over the south. Pet Pardons has grown to more than 500,000 users. Her first rescue Lucky, found a permanent home with a wonderful family as did Capone. Susie and Missy are still looking for their forever family. Sissy was adopted by Kathy Penn, who says her dog is "the freaking best."

Erica Daniel received non-profit status for Dolly's Foundation and quit her job at the shelter to focus on the organization. She found herself in the national spotlight in 2012 after rescuing Harper, a pit bull puppy tossed out as trash. Harper, who suffered from Swimmer Puppy's Syndrome, made a full recovery and appeared with Erica on the Today Show and numerous media outlets. The Daniels kept Harper. In December 2011, Dolly's Foundation helped dogs seized from the Sebring fighting ring outside of Tampa, taking five into its care and assisting several other organizations to place the remaining adoptable dogs into good homes.

*Harper Daniel*

Lilo of Carolina Care Bullies was adopted into a wonderful home; Rae Boney and her family continue to foster. In just two years, Carolina Care Bullies has had 211 adoptions and hosts the annual Pit Bulls in the Park event to offer spay/neuter vouchers, training advice, free micro-chipping and vaccinations to the community.

Jen Carle went to Virginia in August 2011 to help Dogs Deserve Better rebuild Michael Vick's Bad Newz Kennels into a rescue renamed Good Newz Kennels. She continues to sponsor and rehabilitate medical dogs such as Asha, a one year old brindle bully breed that was starved, abused and filled with maggots. After six months of intensive medical treatments, Asha gained 20 pounds and overcame her intense distrust of men. Asha was rescued by Baltimore Bully Crew and is available for adoption. Ava, the sexually abused dog Jen helped rescue, was adopted in June 2012 through Best Friends.

According to Ashley Ferrell, most or all of the dogs Christelle and I met at BARCS were adopted. Unfortunately, Baltimore passed a law in May 2012 that deems pit bull type dogs "inherently vicious," making them at fault in any altercation regardless of the owner or other party's actions. As such, BARCS is now having a harder time adopting out pit bulls, but they are not giving up. BARCS has formed a partnership with trainer Savannah Huff of Pet-U-Cation, who works with specific behavioral problems and evaluates candidates for the "Pit Bull Ambassador" program. Ambassadors must meet or exceed temperament tests such as touch, food guarding, attending adoption events, participate in a play group and must know at least two commands.

Baltimore Bully Crew has saved several more pit bulls, including a sick, mangy mother and her puppies, as well as a 28-pound male hooked onto a 65 lb. chain. Eric personally stepped in and saved the latter dog, which was going to be fought that night. Both are thriving in foster care. Tail's End Kennel in Westminster, Maryland, has donated one-quarter acre of land to Baltimore Bully Crew, which Eric and Kate are building on for use as a fenced-in trail and agility training course for boarding and foster dogs.

Nichole and Aaron Heilbron moved to a home with acreage in Joshua, Texas, with Sachi and Ray, whom they adopted, as well as 8 other dogs. They have added two goats, Fish and Chips, to their menagerie and launched North Texas Pit Bull Advocacy to address the most pressing issues facing pit bulls in their new hometown.

Fawn, the pit mix pup in Indy, found a great home and was renamed Vega. Mended Hearts Indy is now run by Jared and Katie Anderson, with serious assistance from Tara Harvey, Jaimie Carlson, Miranda Paige, Stephanie Herrington and Brandy Bennett. According to Nichole, they have already grown the rescue significantly.

Indy Pit Crew started helping homeless dog owners living in an Indianapolis encampment by offering free food, vaccinations and spay/neuter in June 2012.

Nina Gaither became director of administration for the Indiana War Memorials Foundation. In addition to her many volunteer duties, including Indy Pit Crew, she and Coal greet soldiers returning from duty in Afghanistan and Iraq as part of Welcome Home Dogs.

Safe Humane Chicago's Court Case Dogs has increased the save rate for dogs of criminal owners surrendered to municipal shelters from 2 percent to 50 percent. Of the 154 Court Case dogs, 115 have been adopted, 10 are currently in training and the rest are in foster homes or rescues.

Cincinnati overturned its breed ban in 2012, making it legal for the first time since 2003 for pit bulls to live within city limits.

In 2011, Hello Bully purchased a property north of Pittsburgh. This private location now serves as a Halfway House for Hello Bully's adoptable dogs. Pit Fix Plus continues to be Pittsburgh's only free "speuter" program for Pit Bulls and operates at a rate of more than a dog a day. To date, more than 1,500 dogs have been vaccinated and spayed/neutered through this program.

Mya from the Idaho Falls Shelter found a foster home with a dog trainer shortly after Kara and I departed, while Leonitas, the dog surrendered by the deployed soldier, was adopted. Danyelle Harker now works full-time at the Idaho Falls Shelter as an animal control officer. According to Danyelle, thanks to the remarkable efforts of Shirlene Tomchak and Monica Wright, the Idaho Falls Shelter has not had to euthanize any adoptable dog in many months and has grown its volunteer ranks tremendously. Danyelle and her husband Tollen welcomed their first human child, Easton, into the world on June 2.

My parents Jim and Rosemarie Sathe have moved full time into their RV, traveling the country. You can follow their adventures at www.jimrosietravels.blogspot.com

Charlie Brown, the puppy fostered by the Anderson family in Boise, was adopted by a military family and renamed Tank, only to be returned because of the base's breed ban. Tank has since been adopted by a friend of Julie's and lives on an Oklahoma farm with many acres. He now weighs 70 pounds. Since Tank, the Anderson's have fostered four more pit bulls, including Ayla, who was on her fourth home in four years. An older couple that "never thought they'd own a pit bull" adopted Ayla. She sleeps in their bed.

Cyrus from Nevada Humane Society was taken in by Best Friends Animal Society in the fall of 2011. He lived there for eight months, sharing a kennel with another dog, before succumbing to cancer in April 2012. Trish Hafely was devastated, but also at peace that Cyrus was surrounded by love in his final year.

Diane Blankenburg lost one of her beloved labs, but adopted two more from NHS in his honor: Boomer, a three year old male, and Beignet, a three year old female.

Nevada Humane Society increased its save rate to 93 percent for both dogs and cats in 2011. Cat surrenders were down by 8 percent and overall adoptions increased by 328.

Queenie, my 2010 "Day in Their Paws" partner at The Brittany Foundation, passed on to the rainbow bridge on May 29, 2012. About a dozen volunteers, including myself, came by the ranch to personally kiss her goodbye before she was humanely euthanized due to extreme liver and kidney failure.

## Epilogue & Resources

*Loren and Stefan*

Loren is thriving with Stefan and Lacey. The trio lives in North Hollywood, where Stefan runs two private catering businesses and is a fitness competitor as part of Crossfit High Voltage in Burbank. Stefan's girlfriend, Stephanie Perrin, has fallen in love with Loren and Lacey. Loren's gentle nature has helped Stephanie, who suffered a dog bite injury at six years old that required 60 stitches, overcome her fear of big dogs. Stefan continues to cater "Day in Their Paws" and hosted a "Push Ups for Pups" fundraiser for The Brittany Foundation.

Jake is still the apple of Ashlyn's Burgin's eye. She adopted a female pit bull puppy named Jewel from Castaic Shelter within a year of adopting Jake, who loves being a big brother.

My brother in-law Andy has re-friended me on Facebook and even "likes" some of my pit bull posts now.

AngelDogs Foundation opened its Deaf Dog Rescue in June 2012, taking in deaf dogs from shelters across the country. I'm lucky to spend time with many of them as part of my job and have learned basic hand signals to communicate. In June 2012, AngelDogs Foundation's clinic, thanks to funding from Best Friends No Kill Los Angeles, launched a targeted free spay/neuter program in Pacoima, Panorama City and Sylmar, to fix 1,050 dogs. I have been promoted to program and development director.

"Pit Stops" has sold about 900 copies, so I am one of the 5 percent. After being featured in "Cesar's Way" magazine for the book, I was asked to regularly contribute to its rescue section so I've been able to write about many of the heroes Kara and I met on this trip. As for my diet, I'm sticking to seafood/vegetarian 99 percent of the time, but admit to falling off the wagon a few times and having a couple bites of steak or hamburger. My goal is to someday become a vegan.

Sam, Buster, Sugar, Wayde and I continue as a family, living in the woods. Sam is almost 13 and slowing down, so I'm cherishing every moment with him. His paws will be hard to fill, but when Sam crosses over, I'm for sure getting another pit bull, possibly a deaf one. Sugar Butt is 17 and still rules the house.

*"Hey Mom, are you gonna stick around for a while?"*

Epilogue & Resources

## Resource Directory

**There are many ways you can help pit bulls and homeless pets:**

Always adopt from a shelter or rescue and encourage your friends and family to do so, as well.

If you can't adopt, consider fostering a dog temporarily until they find a home. Most rescues will pay the food and medical costs while a foster pet is in your care.

Volunteer at your local rescue or shelter. Volunteering can include everything from cleaning kennels and walking dogs to helping out at fundraising/adoption events to grant writing, public relations or website development and networking pets through social media.

Donate to your local rescue or shelter, which are always in need of funds or items such as dog food, treats, toys, and blankets.

If you like to drive, offer to transport for your local rescue, which often pull dogs from shelters in other counties or even across the state or the country.

To find an adoptable pet or a shelter or rescue in your community, visit:
www.adoptapet.com
www.petfinder.com

Pit Bull Rescue Central is a nationwide online directory that offers advice on everything from what to do if you find a stray pit bull to how to post private party pit bull adoptions or find an adoptable pit bull in your community. www.pbrc.net

If you suspect someone in your community is involved in dog fighting, report them to the Humane Society of the United States dog fighting hotline at (877) 847-4787. A reward of $5,000 is offered for information leading to the arrest and conviction of a dogfighter. All information is kept confidential.

**To pet owners:**

Please spay and neuter your pets. Not only does spay/neuter stop unwanted animals from entering the world, it provides a multitude of health benefits for your pet.

If you can't keep your pet, responsibly rehome it with a friend, relative or thoroughly screened adopter.

Do not surrender an elderly, sick pet to a municipal shelter, where it will suffer for days before being killed by a stranger. Instead, have your pet humanely put down at your veterinarian's office and be there by his or her side.

**Rescues, Shelters and Advocacy Groups in "Pit Stops 2"**

**California**
AngelDogs Foundation
www.angeldogsfoundation.org
(888) 504-SPAY

The Brittany Foundation
www.brittanyfoundationonline.org

Downtown Dog Rescue
www.downtowndogrescue.org

**Florida**
Dolly's Foundation
www.dollysfoundation.org

## Idaho
Bad Behavior/Good Dog Training (Julie Anderson)
(208) 340-2824

Boise Bully Breed Rescue
www.boisebullybreedrescue.com

Idaho Falls Animal Shelter
2450 Hemmert Avenue
Idaho Falls, ID 83401
(208) 612-8670

## Indiana
Indy Pit Crew
www.indypitcrew.org

Mended Hearts Indy
www.mendedheartsindy.org

## Illinois
Safe Humane Chicago
www.safehumanechicago.org

## Louisiana
Animal Rescue New Orleans
www.animalrescueneworleans.org

If you suspect dog fighting in the New Orleans area, call Crimestoppers Hotline at (504) 822-1111.

## Maryland
Baltimore Animal Rescue and Care Shelter
www.baltimoreanimalshelter.org

Baltimore Bully Crew
www.baltimorebullycrew.com

## Mississippi
Lucky Dog Rescue
www.luckydogrescueblog.blogspot.com

## Nevada
Nevada Humane Society
www.nevadahumanesociety.org

## Pennsylvania
Hello Bully
www.hellobully.com

Western Pennsylvania Humane Society
www.wpahumane.com

If you suspect dog fighting, call the Pennsylvania SPCA Dog Fighting Hotline at (866) 601-SPCA.

## Utah
Best Friends Animal Society
www.bestfriends.org

## Travel Tips
Kara and I stayed almost exclusively at La Quinta Inns and Suites, which are friendly to all breeds of dogs. For more information, visit www.lq.com or call (800) SLEEP-LQ.

A comprehensive listing of dog-friendly lodging, attractions, parks, campgrounds, restaurants and more can be found at www.dogfriendly.com.

For info on great, off-the-beaten path restaurants and diners, visit www.roadfood.com.

When planning a trip with a pit bull, check for breed-specific laws in the cities you wish to visit. Some KOAs and private campgrounds do not allow for bully breeds and other large dogs, so always ask before making a reservation.

For any road trip, always bring along an adequate supply of your pet's regular food and necessary medications, fresh water, leash, collar with ID tag that includes a cell phone number, a crate (optional), and veterinary/vaccination records.

*"I am only one, but still I am one. I cannot do everything, but still I can do something; and because I cannot do everything, I will not refuse to do the something I can do."* ~ *Helen Keller*